maya's secrets

maya's secrets

Delightful Latin Dishes for a Healthier You

Dear Paul
I hope our flavors get
together and we decomplete
a lot for Escoffier.
And also try some of
our Latin flavors
Enjoy!
Maya

Maya León-Meis
Malena Perdomo, MS, RD, CDE
Martín Limas-Villers

American Cancer Society®

Published by the
American Cancer Society/Health Promotions
250 Williams Street NW
Atlanta, Georgia 30303-1002 USA

Printed in the United States of America

Photography: Priscilla Montoya/ArtAgent.com
Cover Photograph: Brian Mark/ArtAgent.com
Food Styling: Elizabeth Hawkins
Design and Composition: rondaflynnwow, inc., Atlanta, GA
Nutritional Analysis: Madelyn Wheeler, MS, RD
Indexing: Bob Land

5　4　3　2　1　　　13　14　15　16　17

Library of Congress Cataloging-in-Publication Data

León-Meis, Maya.
  Maya's secrets : delightful Latin dishes for a healthier you! / Maya León-Meis, Malena Perdomo, Martín Limas-Villers.
    pages cm
  Includes index.
  ISBN 978-1-60443-028-8 (paperback : alk. paper) -- ISBN 1-60443-028-1 (paperback : alk. paper)
  1. Cooking, Latin American. 2. Hispanic Americans--Food. 3. Health promotion. I. Perdomo, Malena. II. Limas-Villers, Martín. III. Title.
  TX716.A1L445 2013
  641.598--dc23
                    2012031382

For more information about cancer, contact your American Cancer Society at **800-227-2345** or **cancer.org**.

Quantity discounts on bulk purchases of this book are available. Book excerpts can also be created to fit specific needs.
For information, please contact your American Cancer Society, Health Promotions Publishing, 250 Williams Street NW, Atlanta, Georgia 30303-1002, or send an e-mail to **trade.sales@cancer.org**.

About the Nutrition Information: The nutrition information shown for each recipe represents one serving. Optional ingredients and ingredients listed without measurement (such as salt and pepper) are not represented in the analysis. When two ingredient choices are given, the first was used in the analysis.

dedications

*To my mom, Yolita, who taught me how to cook
And to the three men in my life: my husband, Tom,
and my two sons, Josh and Chris, who love and appreciate my cooking*
--Maya

*To my mom, Esther Lewis, whom I miss every day; my aunt, Irasema Lewis Epperson,
whom I adore; my grandma, Olimpia Lewis, who taught me how to cook; and to my husband,
Bill Daniels, and my two sons, Alexander and Max, who love my cooking*
--Malena

With love to my parents, Heberto and Hortencía
--Martín

contents

recipe list

Main Dishes

Desserts

introduction

Latin cuisine encompasses a wide assortment of dishes that are influenced by highly diverse regional differences. While there are characteristic qualities and flavors to each region, Latin cuisine is distinctive for its intense flavors, colorful presentation, and variety of spices, which work to create appealing tastes and textures. From the aromatic and sweet, to the tart and piquant flavors of Central and South America, this cookbook has something for everyone.

Eating right doesn't mean that you have to sacrifice flavor. *Maya's Secrets* is all about adapting new and traditional Latin recipes with techniques that not only improve the nutritional value of the dishes, but also make them easy to prepare at home. In these pages, you'll find recipes for appetizers, snacks, soups, sauces, salads, salad dressings, smoothies, sides, main dishes, and desserts, plus a special section featuring child-friendly recipes your kids will love. There's even a section on the most common chilies used in Latin cooking (see pages 2–6).

Looking for healthy versions of traditional delights? Then don't miss our recipes for Pachamanca (page 111), Quick Pozole (page 89), M&M's Refried Beans (page 99), and Vegetarian Tamales (page 133). And that's just the beginning of the delights you'll find here.

At the bottom of each recipe, you'll find nutrition information. Use this information to make healthy, informed, and *balanced* choices throughout the day. We all want to lower our risk of cancer, heart disease, and diabetes. Here are the most important ways to improve your health and reduce your risk of these chronic diseases: don't smoke, watch your weight, stay active, and make healthy food choices. The "American Cancer Society Guidelines on Nutrition and Physical Activity for Cancer Prevention" on page 166 provide important information on the choices everyone can make to improve their overall health.

We know you're busy and that time for cooking is frequently at a premium. Most of the recipes in the book can be prepared quickly, and a number can be made ahead of time or prepared in a slow cooker. To help guide your choices, each recipe includes the time you will need to prepare the ingredients, as well as the total time you'll need to prepare the dish from start to finish.

You will already have some ingredients for these recipes in your cupboard. However, keeping basic Latin ingredients on hand can make a huge difference. See "How to Stock Your Kitchen to Promote Healthy Eating" on pages 162–163 for more help in planning ahead, so you can make a great Latin meal fast.

No matter what you're cooking, there are ways to cut calories and increase nutrients. Take a look at "Recipe Makeovers 101: Three Steps to Healthier Meals," on pages 164–165, for specific tips on making over almost any recipe and ways to incorporate more healthy foods into your life.

These delicious recipes are designed to motivate, captivate, encourage, and inspire. They come from places like Peru, Mexico, Cuba, Panama, and Brazil; some are infused with Mediterranean influences from France, Spain, Italy, and Greece. Some are new, and some are treasured, "secret" family recipes that have been passed down from one generation to the next. Now they're yours.

Enjoy!

common
chilies

CHIPOTLE

SERRANO

POBLANO

HABANERO

JALAPEÑO

ARBOL

ANCHO

ANAHEIM

PERUVIAN YELLOW AJÍ

about chilies

Chilies—hot or mild, sweet or smoked—are an important ingredient in many cuisines in the world and are very important in Latin cooking. Take time to learn about them and experiment with them to add unique flavors to your cooking. The words "chili" and "pepper" are often used interchangeably. Hot peppers can be called "chilies," "peppers," or "chili peppers," whereas mild peppers—bell peppers, for example—are typically just called "peppers." If in doubt, just call it a pepper!

jalapeño

The jalapeño is a fresh chili, green or dark green in color, elongated and conical in shape. It averages 2½ inches long by 1¼ inches wide. It is the most popular and recognizable fresh chili in the United States. When the jalapeño matures, it acquires an intense red color. Jalapeños are hot! To reduce their intensity, jalapeños should be deveined, seeded carefully, and washed. Wear gloves when deveining them. The jalapeño is used in such salsas as Classic Pico de Gallo (page 30). Dried, smoked jalapeños are called chipotle chilies. On a heat scale of 1 to 10, the jalapeño rates a 5 or 6 if not deveined.

chipotle

The chipotle chili is a dried, smoked jalapeño. It is dark reddish brown in color and has a wrinkled texture. On average, the chipotle is 2½ inches long by 1 inch wide. It is one of the hottest dried chilies. In addition to being sold dried, chipotle chilies are commonly sold canned or jarred in a marinade, sauce, or brine, such as in adobo sauce. Chipotles are among the most widely used dried chilies and are considered a must for Mexican cooking. Because they lend a special smoky flavor to soups, rubs, and sauces, they are perfect for barbecue sauces for meats, fish, or poultry. On a heat scale of 1 to 10, chipotles rate 6 or 7.

anaheim

The Anaheim chili is the most common mild green chili available in the United States. It is an elongated, large chili. It can grow to 6 to 10 inches in length and between 1½ and 2 inches wide. The Anaheim is commonly eaten when green, but turns from green to orange when mature. The Anaheim chili can sometimes be hot, though not as hot as the jalapeño. It can be used for chiles rellenos and also in salsas. Dried red Anaheim chilies are used to make ristras (Mexican hanging ornaments). On a heat scale of 1 to 10, the Anaheim chili rates 2 to 3.

poblano

The poblano chili is a large, meaty pepper. It is conical in shape with some undulations. It may resemble a green bell pepper, but it is darker and pointed at the end. It is generally a dark, shiny green, although some varieties may be lighter in color. This chili is relatively mild but may still be too hot for some people. This chili tastes better cooked and should be roasted and peeled before using. The poblano chili is the main ingredient of chiles rellenos. It's also delicious cooked with sour cream and served with chicken or fish. On a heat scale of 1 to 10, the poblano chili rates 3 to 4.

ancho

The ancho chili is a poblano chili that has been dried. In Spanish, *ancho* means wide. It is a triangular-shaped, reddish-brown dry chili with a rough, shiny texture. On average, the ancho chili is about 4½ inches long by 2½ inches wide. It should be flexible and never stiff. When soaked, it acquires a brick-like color. It is the sweetest of the dried chilies. It has a mild fruit flavor, a bit similar to coffee or licorice. It is used to prepare mole sauce, a traditional sauce made with chocolate. On a heat scale of 1 to 10, the ancho chili rates 3 to 4.

serrano

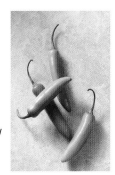

The serrano chili is a small, slim, cylindrical, bullet-shaped chili. On average, it measures 1½ inches wide by 2½ inches long. The serrano changes from medium green to orangeish-red when mature. It can be purchased fresh, but it can also be found canned in serranos en escabeche, a relish of vinegar, onion, carrot, and herbs. Serrano chilies have a distinct fresh citric flavor, great for salsas and guacamole. They do not need to be peeled, but they can be grilled until slightly charred and softened. Serrano chilies are very hot—sometimes up to five times hotter than jalapeños. On a heat scale from 1 to 10, the serrano chili rates 7 to 8.

árbol

The word *árbol* means "tree" in Spanish, and the árbol chili is sometimes called a "tree chili." The árbol chili is a long, thin, green chili that turns a shiny orange-red when mature. It is very hot and is similar to the serrano in taste. On average, it is 2½ inches long by ½ inch wide. It is most commonly used for hot sauces. It can also be toasted until crisp, ground to a powder, and used as a condiment on sliced fruit or vegetables, such as cucumbers or jicama. If the recipe calls for an árbol chili or tree chili and does not specify whether to use fresh or dried, always use a dried chili. Árbol chilies are the small dried red chilies used to decorate holiday wreaths in New Mexico. On a heat scale from 1 to 10, the árbol rates 7 to 8.

habanero

The habanero is one of the hottest chilies. Habanero is pronounced with a silent *h*. Not easily mistaken for other chili peppers, the habanero has a distinctive paper lantern-like shape and orange color. Be careful not to confuse it with the small sweet orange pepper. It is 1 to 2 inches long by 1 to 1½ inches wide. Unripe habaneros are green, and they change color as they mature. Common colors are red and orange, but other colors are sometimes seen. Be extremely careful when handling habaneros, and always use gloves—they are extremely hot. A little bit goes a long way. For instance, if you want to add some kick to a pot of soup, all you have to do is soak one habanero in the soup for a couple of minutes and immediately remove it! On a heat scale of 1 to 10, the habanero chili rates 10!

peruvian yellow ají

The Peruvian yellow ají pepper (ají amarillo) is the king of Peruvian hot chilies. Shaped like the Anaheim chili but yellow with orange tinges, it has a slightly sweet flavor like a yellow bell pepper but is very hot. If the seeds and veins are removed, the degree of heat is tolerable. The ají amarillo adds a very special flavor to traditional dishes, whether used as a seasoning or as a condiment. The traditional Peruvian ají amarillo can sometimes be found jarred in markets that carry Hispanic products. On a heat scale from 1 to 10, the ají amarillo rates 5 to 6, if not deveined and seeded.

how to roast chilies

Roasting fresh chilies softens them, makes it easy to remove the outer skin, and gives them a delicious smoky flavor. Make sure they do not burn completely, or they will be bitter and difficult to work with. Chilies can be roasted over a direct flame, such as a gas burner or grill, or they can be roasted using a "comal" or skillet. A comal is a metal hotplate that is widely used for this purpose in Mexico. Be sure to wear gloves when handling the chilies. Roasted chilies can be used in many different ways, such as in Vegetarian Tamales (page 133), Fettuccine with Poblano Sauce (page 118), and Chilies with Shrimp and Spinach Stuffing (page 114).

1 Place the chilies in a skillet, on a metal hotplate or griddle, on a grill over medium heat, or over a gas burner. Roast for 10 to 15 minutes, turning them to roast on all sides until the peels are brown and blistered.

2 Place chilies in a closed paper or plastic bag for 10 minutes to loosen the skins. Remove the chilies and peel the blistered skins. Wipe off any leftover skin with a damp cloth. Do not rinse the chilies.

3 Cut a slit on one side and remove the seeds carefully to avoid tearing the chilies. If you will be stuffing the chilies, leave the stems on. If you will be using strips of roasted chili, remove the stems, seeds, and membranes.

4 Carefully place the chilies on paper towels and let them dry until ready to use. If stuffing, squeeze lime juice inside the chilies when ready to use.

basic latin salsas& sauces

about sofritos

Sofrito, as it is called in most Latin American countries, or "aderezo," as it is called in Peru, is a cooked base seasoning for a number of Latin dishes. It lends a distinct flavor to stews, soups, pastas, sauces, and other dishes. There is no single recipe for sofrito—each cook has his or her own favorite combination. These are our favorite recipes to make sofrito.

Typically, you would prepare the sofrito and use it immediately. However, you can also chop the ingredients and store them in the refrigerator until ready to sauté, for three to five days. This step will save you a lot of time on busy days and will make it easier, faster, and more practical to cook at home during the week.

maya's sofrito

Sofrito can add wonderful flavor to anything. It could make cardboard taste delicious! Of course, I am kidding, but sofrito truly adds flavor to anything.

Olive oil, 2 tablespoons
Red or yellow onion, 1, finely chopped
Garlic, 1 clove, minced
Ground cumin, ¼ teaspoon
Salt, ¼ teaspoon
Ground black pepper, ¼ teaspoon

Cook the onion in the oil until translucent. Add the rest of the ingredients and cook until softened.

malena's sofrito

I like to prep all the ingredients and then wait to cook the mixture until I'm ready to use it. You can use a food processor to chop the vegetables if you like—just don't overprocess the vegetables. I use sofrito when I'm preparing rice recipes and also to marinate fish, chicken, and meat.

Olive oil, 1 tablespoon
Onion, ½, finely chopped
Cilantro leaves, chopped, 1 cup
Celery, 1 long stalk, chopped
Green bell pepper, 1, stemmed, seeded, and coarsely chopped

Cook the onion in the oil until translucent. Add the rest of the ingredients and cook until softened.

martín's sofrito

I like to use sofrito for any kind of stew or soup, all sorts of meat dishes, and even with beans.

Olive oil, 2 tablespoons
Onion, ½, finely chopped
Garlic, 2 cloves, finely chopped
Jalapeño, 1, seeded, deveined, and diced
Salt and ground black pepper

Cook the onion in the oil until translucent. Add the rest of the ingredients and cook until softened.

mexican-style green salsa

Jalapeños, 2 to 3, stemmed, or to taste

Tomatillos, 6 (approximately 1 pound), husks removed, rinsed

Garlic, 1 clove

Salt, ½ teaspoon

This is one of the most traditional sauces in Mexico, and it is widely used in the United States in many Mexican dishes. It is used as a condiment for tacos, burritos, enchiladas, seafood dishes, meats, and even as a dip. This recipe is very healthy because it only calls for fresh vegetables. Tomatillos (pronounced tohm-a-tee-yohs) are found in the produce areas in most general supermarkets and in Hispanic markets. They look like green tomatoes with papery husks. Remove the husks before cooking.
—Malena

Prep Time: 5 minutes | Total Time: 20 minutes | Makes about 3 cups

1 Place the jalapeños and tomatillos in a pan with water to cover. Over high heat, bring to a boil and cook for 2 minutes. Reduce heat to medium, cover, and cook for an additional 5 to 10 minutes.

2 When tomatillos have changed from green to yellow, drain the tomatillos and the jalapeños.

3 Transfer to a blender or food processor. Add garlic and salt and blend for 1 minute. Use immediately or store in the refrigerator. The salsa can be served warm or cold.

Per Serving (about ¼ cup)
Calories, 15
Total fat, 0.4 g
   Saturated fat, 0.1 g
   Trans fat, 0.0 g
   Polyunsaturated fat, 0.2 g
   Monounsaturated fat, 0.1 g
Total carbohydrate, 3 g
   Dietary fiber, 1 g
   Sugars, 2 g
Protein, 1 g
Sodium, 98 mg

roasted tomato salsa

This tomato salsa is great with homemade tortilla chips or as a condiment for grilled meats, chicken, or fish. It is really worthwhile to have fresh salsa at home! Instead of using Roma tomatoes, one variation for this recipe is to roast tomatillos. Remove the papery husks and rinse to remove the stickiness before roasting. The rest of the preparation is the same. Roasted or raw jalapeño or serrano chilies may be added to the blender when making the salsa. Play with the flavors and create your own variations!
—Martín

Roma tomatoes, 4 to 5 (approximately 1 pound)

Garlic, 2 cloves, unpeeled

Jalapeños, 1 to 3, or 1 serrano chili, stemmed, seeded, and deveined

Yellow onion, ½ medium

Water, ½ cup

Canola oil, 1 tablespoon

Salt, ½ teaspoon

Prep Time: 20 minutes | Total Time: 40 minutes | Makes about 2½ cups

1 Place the tomatoes and garlic in a skillet or comal over medium heat. Roast the tomatoes and garlic, turning them over to cook on all sides. Remove the garlic after 2 minutes, or when browned. It should still be firm.

2 Continue cooking the tomatoes for 8 to 10 minutes, or until the peels are soft and darkened. Remove tomatoes from heat.

3 In a blender or food processor, purée the tomatoes, garlic, jalapeños, and onion with ½ cup of water.

4 Heat oil in a skillet and add the puréed mixture. Bring to a boil, lower heat, and simmer for 5 to 10 minutes. Add salt, stir, and remove from heat. Taste and adjust seasoning as necessary. Serve warm or at room temperature.

Pan-roasting tomatoes takes some time, but the unique smoked flavor is unbeatable. Use a skillet or comal, a metal hotplate widely used in Mexico. The tomato skin will blister and slightly burn in some areas.

Per Serving (about ¼ cup)
Calories, 25
Total fat, 1.5 g
    Saturated fat, 0.1 g
    Trans fat, 0.0 g
    Polyunsaturated fat, 0.4 g
    Monounsaturated fat, 0.9 g
Total carbohydrate, 3 g
    Dietary fiber, 1 g
    Sugars, 2 g
Protein, 1 g
Sodium, 120 mg

peruvian creole sauce

Red onion, 1, julienned

Salt, 1 teaspoon

Cilantro leaves, chopped, 2 tablespoons

Red wine vinegar, 1 tablespoon

Juice of 1 lime

Extra-virgin olive oil, 1 tablespoon

Cayenne pepper, to taste

This traditional sauce of pickled onions was always on our table at home when I was young. We used it as a condiment to add a unique flavor to such dishes as arroz con pollo (rice and chicken), boiled or baked potatoes, sandwiches, and bean dishes. I learned this recipe from my mom, who was a fabulous cook. —Maya

Prep Time: 10 minutes | Total Time: 30 minutes | Makes about 1¼ cups

1 Place the sliced onion in a fine mesh colander and add salt. Toss to coat and set aside for 5 to 10 minutes.

2 Rinse the onion in cold running water and drain well.

3 Transfer the onion to a glass bowl and add the remaining ingredients.

4 Mix well and marinate for 10 to 15 minutes before serving. Serve immediately.

Per Serving (about ¼ cup)
Calories, 38
Total fat, 2.7 g
   Saturated fat, 0.4 g
   Trans fat, 0.0 g
   Polyunsaturated fat, 0.3 g
   Monounsaturated fat, 2.0 g
Total carbohydrate, 3 g
   Dietary fiber, 1 g
   Sugars, 1 g
Protein, 0 g
Sodium, 30 mg

"almost true" peruvian yellow hot pepper sauce

Traditional Peruvian yellow hot pepper sauce is a basic ingredient for a number of Peruvian dishes. Made from the ají chili, this sauce gives dishes a spicy kick and unique flavor. True Peruvian yellow hot pepper sauce can be hard to find in the United States, so I created this version, which does not need ají chilies and is almost like tasting the original.
—Maya

Canola oil, 3 tablespoons

Yellow bell pepper, 1 large, stemmed, seeded, and coarsely chopped

White onion, ½, coarsely chopped

Garlic, 1 clove

Kosher salt, ½ teaspoon, or to taste

Apple cider vinegar, 1 teaspoon

Yellow mustard, 1 tablespoon

Sugar, 1 teaspoon

Cayenne pepper, ¼ teaspoon, or to taste

Prep Time: 10 minutes | Total Time: 15 minutes | Makes about ½ cup

1 Heat the canola oil in a heavy skillet. Cook the yellow bell pepper and onion over medium-high heat for about 2 to 3 minutes or until brown, stirring constantly. Add the garlic and the salt and continue cooking for about a minute.

2 Pour the mixture into a blender and blend well.

3 Add the apple cider vinegar, mustard, and sugar and blend well. Taste and add cayenne pepper.

4 Serve immediately or store in a glass jar with a plastic lid in the refrigerator for five to seven days.

This sauce can also be used as a condiment for boiled or baked potatoes; roasted chicken, meat, or fish; meat kabobs; corn on the cob; sandwiches; and various appetizers.

Per Serving (about 1 tablespoon)
Calories, 48
Total fat, 4.3 g
    Saturated fat, 0.3 g
    Trans fat, 0.0 g
    Polyunsaturated fat, 1.2 g
    Monounsaturated fat, 2.7 g
Total carbohydrate, 3 g
    Dietary fiber, 0 g
    Sugars, 1 g
Protein, 0 g
Sodium, 114 mg

homemade tomato sauce

Tomatoes, 8 (approximately 2 pounds), stemmed

Red onion, 1 medium, quartered

Garlic, 3 cloves

Red bell pepper, 1, stemmed, seeded, and coarsely chopped

Dark brown sugar, 1 tablespoon

Reduced-sodium soy sauce, 2 tablespoons

Bay leaves, 2

Dried oregano, 1 teaspoon

Red wine, ¼ cup

This versatile tomato sauce can be used in lots of different ways, including some recipes you will find in this book. To make a marinara-style spaghetti sauce, add Italian seasoning to taste. For a chicken dish, use chicken seasoning instead. You can add mushrooms, more peppers, or increase the amount of garlic—it's up to you. This sauce can last about three weeks when refrigerated. It can also be frozen in small portions and defrosted as needed. —Malena

Prep Time: 20 minutes | Total Time: 1 hour | Makes about 6 cups

1 With a sharp knife, cut a shallow cross-shaped slit in the top of each tomato.

2 Fill a 4-quart pot with water and bring to a boil. Immerse the tomatoes in the boiling water for 1 minute. Remove them and allow them to cool. Once cool, remove the skins.

3 Place the tomatoes, onion, garlic, and red pepper in a blender or food processor and blend thoroughly.

4 Place the vegetable mixture in a pot and place over high heat. Add the brown sugar, soy sauce, bay leaves, and oregano, and bring to a boil. Cook for 8 to 10 minutes. Lower the heat, add the red wine, and simmer for at least 30 minutes and up to 2 hours, stirring occasionally.

5 Remove bay leaves. Use immediately or store in the refrigerator or freezer.

Per Serving (about ½ cup)
Calories, 37
Total fat, 0.2 g
    Saturated fat, 0.0 g
    Trans fat, 0.0 g
    Polyunsaturated fat, 0.0 g
    Monounsaturated fat, 0.0 g
Total carbohydrate, 6 g
    Dietary fiber, 1 g
    Sugars, 4 g
Protein, 1 g
Sodium, 101 mg

white sauce (béchamel sauce)

This classic French sauce is now part of a variety of Latin American dishes. It needs to be used immediately after it is prepared. You can also add garlic, grated cheese, chopped basil, chopped parsley, or spinach. Use this sauce to prepare Flounder Stuffed with Crabmeat (page 110), Vegetarian Lasagna (page 129), and Peruvian Covered Rice (page 125). —Maya

Unsalted butter, 2 tablespoons

All-purpose flour, 2 tablespoons, sifted

Milk (2 percent), 1 cup, warmed

Salt, ½ teaspoon

Nutmeg, ⅛ teaspoon, freshly grated

Ground white pepper, ¼ teaspoon

Prep Time: 5 minutes | Total Time: 20 minutes | Makes about 1 cup

1 Melt the butter in a medium saucepan over medium heat, watching it to prevent burning. Slowly add the flour and use a wooden spoon to stir constantly until the mixture is smooth and slightly golden in color, approximately 2 minutes.

2 Gradually add the warm milk to the mixture. Stir constantly to prevent lumps from forming until the mixture is totally smooth.

3 When it starts bubbling, lower the heat and simmer for 3 to 5 minutes, stirring constantly.

4 Season with salt, nutmeg, and white pepper. Mix well and remove from heat. Set aside until ready to use. To prevent a skin from forming on the top, cover until it cools off a little and then press a sheet of plastic wrap directly onto the top of the white sauce.

5 When ready to use, stir well. If the sauce has become too thick, add more warm milk and stir well.

Per Serving (about ¼ cup)
Calories, 97
Total fat, 7.0 g
    Saturated fat, 4.4 g
    Trans fat, 0.2 g
    Polyunsaturated fat, 0.3 g
    Monounsaturated fat, 2.1 g
Total carbohydrate, 6 g
    Dietary fiber, 0 g
    Sugars, 3 g
Protein, 3 g
Sodium, 370 mg

appetizers & snacks

peruvian ceviche

Firm white fish (such as catfish, sea bass, or red snapper), 1 pound

Red onion, 1, thinly sliced

Salt, 1 tablespoon plus ½ teaspoon, divided

Peruvian yellow (ají) pepper, ½ to 1, stemmed, seeded, deveined, and chopped, or a pinch cayenne pepper

Juice of 6 to 8 limes (about 1½ cups)

Ground black pepper, ¼ teaspoon, or to taste

Cilantro leaves, chopped, 2 tablespoons

Garlic, crushed, 1 teaspoon

This traditional Peruvian dish is refreshing and delicious. Catfish, sea bass, and red snapper all work well in this recipe. You can add other types of seafood, such as scallops or shrimp. If you are using shellfish, cook it lightly first by pouring boiling water over it in a colander. Sprinkling the red onion with salt will soften it a bit.

You can usually find Peruvian yellow ají peppers in jars at Hispanic markets. If you can't find them, substitute a pinch of cayenne pepper. Serve this dish over lettuce leaves with sliced, boiled sweet potato or yam on the side. —Maya

Prep Time: 30 minutes | Total Time: 3 hours | **4 Servings**

1 Wash the fish and cut into bite-sized cubes. Place the fish in a glass container.

2 Place the sliced red onion in a fine mesh colander. Add 1 tablespoon of the salt and toss to coat. Let sit for 5 minutes. Rinse well with fresh water and set aside.

3 Purée the ají peppers in a blender. In a bowl, combine the puréed ají peppers, lime juice, salt, black pepper, cilantro, and garlic. Taste and adjust flavoring as desired.

4 Pour the mixture over the fish, making sure it is covered completely. Stir well to coat evenly.

5 Place the onion on top of the fish. Let the fish marinate in the refrigerator for at least 2 to 3 hours. Mix well before serving.

Ceviche is made by marinating seafood in a citrus mixture, most often lime juice or lemon juice. The citric acid changes the structure of the proteins in the seafood, "cooking" the fish without using heat. The fish will change from transparent when raw to solid white when pickled. It is important that you use fresh lime or lemon juice.

Per Serving
Calories, 192
Total fat, 8.0 g
    Saturated fat, 1.9 g
    Trans fat, 0.0 g
    Polyunsaturated fat, 1.5 g
    Monounsaturated fat, 4.3 g
Total carbohydrate, 10 g
    Dietary fiber, 1 g
    Sugars, 3 g
Protein, 20 g
Sodium, 406 mg

beach ceviche

This recipe is called "Beach Ceviche" because in Lima, Peru, it's prepared on site, often at the beach or the countryside. At home, it's quick and easy to prepare and tastes great! —Maya

Prep Time: 15 minutes | **Total Time:** 15 minutes | **4 Servings**

1 Put the tuna in a glass bowl and add the lime juice, salt, black pepper, and cayenne pepper.

2 Add the onion and stir to combine. Taste and add more lime juice, salt, or pepper if necessary.

3 Add the tomatoes and stir gently to combine.

4 Stuff a leaf of lettuce with the tuna mixture to eat the ceviche taco-style, or simply put the ceviche mixture on a leaf of lettuce to serve it like a salad.

Chunk light tuna packed in water, 1 (12-ounce) can, drained

Juice of 3 to 4 limes

Salt, pinch

Ground black pepper, ¼ teaspoon, or to taste

Cayenne pepper, pinch, optional

Red onion, ½, finely chopped

Tomatoes, 2, chopped

Romaine lettuce, 4 leaves

Per Serving
Calories, 96
Total fat, 0.9 g
    Saturated fat, 0.2 g
    Trans fat, 0.0 g
    Polyunsaturated fat, 0.4 g
    Monounsaturated fat, 0.2 g
Total carbohydrate, 8 g
    Dietary fiber, 2 g
    Sugars, 3 g
Protein, 16 g
Sodium, 256 mg

panamanian ceviche

For a recipe such as ceviche, which is highly acidic, it is important to use a nonreactive bowl. Aluminum, cast iron, and copper are all "reactive" and can give the food a metallic flavor. Glass, ceramic, stainless steel, and metal cookware with enamel coating are "nonreactive." Nonreactive materials do not react with food and will not affect the flavors of the dish.

Serve with whole grain crackers or homemade tortilla chips. This ceviche is always a big hit at my parties. —Malena

Halibut, skinless, 1 pound

Malena's Sofrito (page 10), 2 tablespoons

Red or yellow onion, ½ medium, finely chopped

Celery, ½ stalk, finely chopped (about 2 tablespoons)

Cilantro leaves, coarsely chopped, 1 tablespoon

Juice of 6 to 8 limes (about 1½ cups)

Salt, ½ teaspoon

Hot sauce, ½ teaspoon, or ½ serrano **chili,** seeded, deveined, and finely chopped, optional

Prep Time: 30 minutes | **Total Time:** 3 hours to overnight (including refrigeration) | **4 Servings**

1 Wash the fish and cut into bite-sized cubes. Remove any bones.

2 Combine the fish, sofrito, onion, celery, cilantro, lime juice, salt, and hot sauce in a glass container with a lid. Make sure the lime juice covers the fish completely, adding more if necessary.

3 Refrigerate for at least 2 to 3 hours. The ceviche is best if prepared the night before serving, though it can be eaten when the fish turns from translucent to solid white. Before serving, taste and add more salt, if necessary.

Per Serving
Calories, 152
Total fat, 3.1 g
    Saturated fat, 0.4 g
    Trans fat, 0.0 g
    Polyunsaturated fat, 0.9 g
    Monounsaturated fat, 1.0 g
Total carbohydrate, 8 g
    Dietary fiber, 1 g
    Sugars, 2 g
Protein, 24 g
Sodium, 371 mg

mushroom and avocado ceviche

Water, 4 cups

Salt

Limes, 3, divided

Mushrooms, 1 pound, sliced

Cilantro leaves, chopped, ¼ cup

Red onion, ¼, chopped

Cucumber, ½, peeled, seeded, and chopped

Tomatoes, 3, seeded and chopped

Avocados, 2, peeled, pitted, and cubed

Serrano chilies, 2, stemmed, seeded, deveined, and chopped, or to taste

Dried oregano, ¼ teaspoon

This appetizer is delicious served with whole wheat saltine crackers or another cracker of your choice. —Martín

Prep Time: 20 minutes | **Total Time:** 25 minutes | **8 Servings**

1 In a medium saucepan, combine 4 cups water with a pinch of salt and the juice of half a lime and bring to a boil. Add the mushrooms and cook for 1 minute. Remove, drain, and set aside.

2 In a glass container, combine the mushrooms, cilantro, onion, cucumber, tomatoes, avocados, and chilies.

3 Add the juice from the remaining limes and the oregano and mix thoroughly. Add salt, if necessary. Refrigerate until ready to serve.

Per Serving
Calories, 89
Total fat, 5.9 g
    Saturated fat, 0.8 g
    Trans fat, 0.0 g
    Polyunsaturated fat, 0.8 g
    Monounsaturated fat, 3.7 g
Total carbohydrate, 9 g
    Dietary fiber, 4 g
    Sugars, 3 g
Protein, 3 g
Sodium, 12 mg

tuna dip

Serve this dip as a snack with whole wheat crackers or veggies of your choice. This recipe is from Carmita, a very good Cuban friend of mine from whom I learned not only delicious recipes but very wise life lessons. That is why I call her my "Cuban mother." —Maya

Chunk light tuna packed in water, 1 (12-ounce) can, drained

Reduced-fat mayonnaise, 3 tablespoons

Yellow mustard, 1 teaspoon

Ground black pepper, to taste

Prep Time: 5 minutes | **Total Time:** 5 minutes | **Makes about 1 cup**

1 Blend all the ingredients in a food processor until perfectly smooth.

Per Serving (about ¼ cup)
Calories, 99
Total fat, 4.1 g
    Saturated fat, 0.7 g
    Trans fat, 0.0 g
    Polyunsaturated fat, 2.1 g
    Monounsaturated fat, 1.0 g
Total carbohydrate, 1 g
    Dietary fiber, 0 g
    Sugars, 1 g
Protein, 15 g
Sodium, 348 mg

hummus

Chickpeas, 1 (15-ounce) can, drained

Low-fat plain yogurt, ½ cup

Tahini, 1 tablespoon

Garlic, 1 clove

Freshly squeezed lime juice, 1 tablespoon

Extra-virgin olive oil, 2 tablespoons

Paprika, 1 teaspoon

Dried oregano, pinch

Salt, ½ teaspoon, or to taste

Serve this hummus with toasted whole wheat pita bread cut into triangles, or eat it with fresh carrots, cucumber, celery, jicama, and other vegetables. Tahini is a paste made of sesame seeds. It can be found jarred in most supermarkets. This dish makes a great appetizer or mid-afternoon snack. —Malena

Prep Time: 10 minutes | **Total Time:** 10 minutes | **Makes about 2 cups**

1 Combine all the ingredients in a food processor and mix for 2 minutes until smooth. Add salt to taste.

Per Serving (about ⅓ cup)
Calories, 138
Total fat, 7.3 g
    Saturated fat, 1.1 g
    Trans fat, 0.0 g
    Polyunsaturated fat, 1.6 g
    Monounsaturated fat, 4.1 g
Total carbohydrate, 14 g
    Dietary fiber, 4 g
    Sugars, 4 g
Protein, 5 g
Sodium, 283 mg

guacamole

This guacamole is delicious served with homemade tortilla chips or as a dip for fresh vegetables. See the recipe for baked tortilla chips included with the recipe for Classic Pico de Gallo on page 30. If you don't have serrano chilies, you can use one jalapeño or a few drops of hot sauce instead. If you prefer less spice, simply omit the chilies. —Martin

Prep Time: 10 to 15 minutes | **Total Time:** 10 to 15 minutes | **Makes about 2 cups**

1 Rub the garlic clove inside the bowl where the guacamole will be mixed. Discard the garlic.

2 Cut the avocados in half, discard the pits, and scrape the flesh into the bowl. Add the onion and mix until it forms a paste-like consistency.

3 Add the cilantro, tomato, serrano chilies, and lime juice. Stir and season with salt.

Garlic, 1 clove

Avocados, 2, ripe

Onion, finely chopped, ¼ cup

Cilantro leaves, chopped, ¼ cup

Tomato, 1 large, chopped

Serrano chilies, 1 to 2, stemmed, seeded, deveined, and finely chopped, optional

Juice of 1 lime

Salt, ½ teaspoon, or to taste

Per Serving (about ¼ cup)
Calories, 68
Total fat, 5.6 g
    Saturated fat, 0.8 g
    Trans fat, 0.0 g
    Polyunsaturated fat, 0.7 g
    Monounsaturated fat, 3.7 g
Total carbohydrate, 5 g
    Dietary fiber, 3 g
    Sugars, 1 g
Protein, 1 g
Sodium, 150 mg

tomato surprise

Chunk light tuna packed in water,
1 (12-ounce) can, drained

Red onion, finely chopped, ½ cup

Avocado, 1, peeled, pitted, and cubed

Juice of 1 to 2 limes

Salt and ground black pepper, to taste

Tomatoes, 6 large, ripe but firm

My mom used to prepare this dish on Sundays. Our family was always delighted with it because it gave our meal a festive touch. —Maya

Prep Time: 20 minutes | **Total Time:** 20 minutes | **6 Servings**

1 Combine the tuna, onion, avocado, and juice of one lime in a glass bowl. Taste and add salt, pepper, or additional lime juice as desired. Set aside.

2 Wash the tomatoes and cut off the top of each one to make a small lid. Gently scoop the pulp and seeds out of the tomatoes with a paring knife and a spoon.

3 Fill tomatoes with the tuna mixture and top with the tomato lid.

Per Serving
Calories, 120
Total fat, 4.4 g
    Saturated fat, 0.7 g
    Trans fat, 0.0 g
    Polyunsaturated fat, 0.8 g
    Monounsaturated fat, 2.6 g
Total carbohydrate, 11 g
    Dietary fiber, 4 g
    Sugars, 5 g
Protein, 12 g
Sodium, 174 mg

American Cancer Society

classic pico de gallo

Tomatoes, 4, seeded and chopped

Onion, 1, finely chopped

Cilantro leaves, finely chopped, ½ cup

Serrano chilies or jalapeños, 2 to 3, stemmed, seeded, deveined, and finely chopped

Freshly squeezed lime juice, ¼ cup

Olive oil, 1 tablespoon

Salt and ground black pepper, to taste

To make your own homemade tortilla chips, cut corn tortillas into triangles and place them on a baking sheet. Spray lightly with nonstick cooking spray and bake for 5 minutes in a 400 degree oven. The tortilla chips can also be baked in a toaster oven.

The serrano or jalapeño chilies give this salsa a nice kick, but they are optional. —Martín

Prep Time: 15 minutes | **Total Time:** 15 minutes | **Makes about 3 cups**

1 In a glass bowl, mix the tomatoes, onion, cilantro, chilies, lime juice, and olive oil. Season with salt and pepper to taste. Serve immediately.

Per Serving
Calories, 48
Total fat, 2.5 g
    Saturated fat, 0.3 g
    Trans fat, 0.0 g
    Polyunsaturated fat, 0.3 g
    Monounsaturated fat, 1.7 g
Total carbohydrate, 7 g
    Dietary fiber, 2 g
    Sugars, 4 g
Protein, 1 g
Sodium, 8 mg

beef turnovers

For me, the most delicious and healthy dough for turnovers is from my Aunt Irasema. We've included her recipe on page 35. You can also use ground turkey breast in this recipe to make it even lower in fat.
—Malena

Prep Time: 25 minutes | Total Time: 1 hour and 15 minutes | **12 Servings** (one turnover each)

1 Preheat the oven to 375 degrees.

2 Heat the oil in a nonstick frying pan over medium-high heat and sauté the onion and tomato for 2 minutes. Add the ground beef and cook for an additional 5 minutes, stirring frequently, or until the meat is thoroughly browned. Add chopped parsley and cilantro.

3 Once the meat is browned, tilt the pan and spoon off the excess liquid or grease. Reduce heat and add tomato sauce, ketchup, and red wine. Mix well and add salt and pepper to taste.

4 Continue to cook for about 5 to 10 minutes, or until most of the liquid has evaporated. Add the raisins and olives. Mix well. Remove from the heat and set aside while you prepare the dough.

5 Prepare the dough according to the recipe on page 35.

6 To assemble the turnovers, place a tablespoon of filling in the center of each piece of dough. Brush a small amount of water along the edges of each turnover and fold in half. Pinch the edges together with your fingers.

7 Place the turnovers on a baking sheet coated with nonstick cooking spray. Use the tines of a fork to completely seal the turnovers all along the edges. Mix the egg yolk with a tablespoon of milk or water and brush over the top of each turnover.

8 Bake for 20 minutes or until golden brown.

Canola oil, 1 tablespoon

Onion, finely chopped, ½ cup

Tomato, 1 large, chopped

Lean ground beef (95 percent lean) or ground turkey breast, 1 pound

Flat leaf parsley, chopped, ⅓ cup

Cilantro leaves, chopped, ⅓ cup

Tomato sauce, 1 (8-ounce) can

Ketchup, 1 tablespoon

Red wine, 2 tablespoons

Salt and ground black pepper, to taste

Raisins, 2 tablespoons

Green olives, chopped, 2 tablespoons

Aunt Irasema's Turnover Dough (page 35)

Egg yolk, 1

Milk or water, 1 tablespoon

Per Serving
Calories, 167
Total fat, 4.7 g
    Saturated fat, 1.2 g
    Trans fat, 0.1 g
    Polyunsaturated fat, 0.8 g
    Monounsaturated fat, 2.4 g
Total carbohydrate, 20 g
    Dietary fiber, 1 g
    Sugars, 3 g
Protein, 10 g
Sodium, 302 mg

tropical cocktail

This recipe is perfect for parties. For a festive touch, you can garnish with a few shrimp hooked over the glass's edge. The imitation crabmeat in this recipe can be replaced with a half pound of cooked, peeled medium shrimp. This dish is also delicious with homemade tortilla chips.—Maya

Prep Time: 30 minutes | **Total Time:** 1 hour to 1 hour and 30 minutes | **8 Servings**

1 Combine all the ingredients in a large glass bowl and mix well. Marinate for 30 to 60 minutes in the refrigerator.

2 Taste and adjust seasoning or add more lime juice as desired.

Tomato and clam cocktail juice, 1 (32-ounce) bottle

Imitation crabmeat, 1 pound

Green bell pepper, 1, stemmed, seeded, and diced

Red bell pepper, 1, stemmed, seeded, and diced

Tomatoes, 2, diced

Avocados, 2, peeled, pitted, and diced

Cucumbers, 2, peeled and diced

Juice of 4 limes

Garlic, minced, ¼ teaspoon

Salt and ground black pepper, to taste

Cilantro leaves, chopped, ¼ cup

Apple cider vinegar, 1 teaspoon

Per Serving
Calories, 165
Total fat, 6.1 g
    Saturated fat, 1.0 g
    Trans fat, 0.0 g
    Polyunsaturated fat, 0.9 g
    Monounsaturated fat, 3.8 g
Total carbohydrate, 23 g
    Dietary fiber, 5 g
    Sugars, 12 g
Protein, 7 g
Sodium, 922 mg

savory vegetable and cheese turnovers

Olive oil, 1 tablespoon

White onion, ½, finely sliced

Garlic, 2 cloves, minced

Red or green bell pepper, 1, stemmed, seeded, and finely chopped

Chayote, 1, halved, cored, and diced

Carrots, shredded, 1 cup

Salt and ground black pepper, to taste

Juice of 1 lime, optional

Roasted Tomato Salsa (page 13), 1 cup, or 1 cup store-bought roasted tomato salsa, divided, optional

Aunt Irasema's Turnover Dough (page 35)

Swiss cheese, 6 slices, diced

Egg yolk, 1

Milk or water, 1 tablespoon

One of the vegetables used in this recipe is chayote, a native Mexican plant and member of the squash family. It has a mild, crisp flavor. In this turnover filling, it's mixed with other vegetables and Swiss cheese for an exquisite savory treat. Fresh chard can also be added. —Malena

Prep Time: 25 minutes | **Total Time:** 1 hour | **12 Servings** (one turnover each)

1 Preheat the oven to 375 degrees.

2 In a skillet or wok with a sturdy bottom, heat the olive oil over medium-high heat. Add all the vegetables and sauté, stirring frequently, until the vegetables are tender. Add salt and pepper. Add the lime juice and ¾ cup of the salsa and stir until well combined. Taste and add more salsa, salt, or pepper, if needed. Remove from heat and set aside.

3 Prepare the dough according to the recipe on page 35.

4 Place a tablespoon of filling in the center of each piece of dough and top with a few pieces of cheese. Brush a small amount of water along the edges of each turnover and fold in half. Pinch the edges together with your fingers.

5 Spray a baking sheet with nonstick cooking spray. Place the turnovers on the baking sheet and use the tines of a fork to seal the turnovers all along the edges. Mix the egg yolk with a tablespoon of milk and brush over the top of each turnover.

6 Bake for 20 minutes or until golden brown.

Per Serving
Calories, 167
Total fat, 6.5 g
   Saturated fat, 2.9 g
   Trans fat, 0.1 g
   Polyunsaturated fat, 0.7 g
   Monounsaturated fat, 2.5 g
Total carbohydrate, 21 g
   Dietary fiber, 2 g
   Sugars, 2 g
Protein, 7 g
Sodium, 178 mg

aunt irasema's turnover dough

This is my Aunt Irasema's recipe. She prepares her own dough so that she knows exactly what goes into it, and I prefer it to any other dough! It's also healthier as it contains only a small amount of fat. Use this dough to prepare meat or vegetable turnovers (pages 31 and 34).
—Malena

All-purpose flour, 2 cups

Baking powder, 1½ teaspoons

Salt, ½ teaspoon

Sugar, ½ teaspoon

Warm water, ¾ cup

Canola or vegetable oil, 2 teaspoons

Prep Time: 15 minutes | **Total Time:** 20 minutes | **12 Servings**

1 Preheat the oven to 375 degrees.

2 Place all the dry ingredients for the dough in a large bowl and add ¾ cup warm water and canola oil.

3 Use a plastic spatula to combine the ingredients, moving what sticks to the bowl to the center of the dough. Next, use your hands to mix thoroughly. Form the dough into a large ball. You can add extra water, a teaspoon at a time, if the dough is too dry.

4 Place the dough on a floured surface. Flatten with a rolling pin until the dough is about ⅛-inch thick.

5 Using a cutter or a 4-inch diameter can or cup, cut twelve circles. After cutting, stretch each circle by hand, turning the dough on your palms until it is sufficiently thin. Follow the recipes on pages 31 and 34 to make turnovers.

Per Serving
Calories, 83
Total fat, 1.0 g
   Saturated fat, 0.1 g
   Trans fat, 0.0 g
   Polyunsaturated fat, 0.3 g
   Monounsaturated fat, 0.5 g
Total carbohydrate, 16 g
   Dietary fiber, 1 g
   Sugars, 1 g
Protein, 2 g
Sodium, 143 mg

peruvian-style russian salad

Beets, 2, cooked, or 1 (8.5-ounce) can beets, drained and cubed

Frozen peas and carrots, 2 cups, thawed and drained, or 2 (8.5-ounce) cans peas and carrots, drained

Reduced-fat mayonnaise, ¼ cup

Freshly squeezed lime juice, 2 tablespoons

Salt, ¼ teaspoon, or to taste

Ground black pepper, ¼ teaspoon, or to taste

Serve this salad as an appetizer or snack with whole grain crackers or stuffed in avocados cut in half. You can also add a can of tuna for a more filling salad. —Maya

Prep Time: 10 minutes | **Total Time:** 20 minutes | **4 Servings**

1 Combine all ingredients in a glass bowl and mix well.

Per Serving
Calories, 109
Total fat, 5.3 g
    Saturated fat, 0.8 g
    Trans fat, 0.0 g
    Polyunsaturated fat, 2.9 g
    Monounsaturated fat, 1.2 g
Total carbohydrate, 12 g
    Dietary fiber, 3 g
    Sugars, 7 g
Protein, 3 g
Sodium, 354 mg

juices & smoothies

pear and strawberry smoothie

Bartlett pear, 1, unpeeled, cored, and sliced, or 1 (11-ounce) can sliced pears packed in 100 percent juice, drained

Strawberries, 2, hulled

Crushed ice, ½ cup

Nonfat plain yogurt, ⅓ cup

Milk (skim), ⅓ cup

Honey, 1 teaspoon

Water, ½ cup

This delicious and light smoothie is one of my favorites. I like to substitute orange juice and a squeeze of lime juice for the milk and yogurt in this recipe for a different flavor. —Martin

Prep Time: 5 minutes | **Total Time:** 5 minutes | **2 Servings** (1 cup each)

1 Place all the ingredients in a blender and blend well. Serve immediately.

For added flavor, you can substitute apple juice or green tea for the water. To add flavor and nutrition, you can add our Quinoa and Apple Smoothie Booster (page 45), flaxseed meal, protein powder, peanut butter, almond butter, or other fruits, such as bananas.

Per Serving
Calories, 96
Total fat, 0.2 g
  Saturated fat, 0.1 g
  Trans fat, 0.0 g
  Polyunsaturated fat, 0.0 g
  Monounsaturated fat, 0.1 g
Total carbohydrate, 22 g
  Dietary fiber, 3 g
  Sugars, 16 g
Protein, 4 g
Sodium, 47 mg

maya's "wonder juice"

When I was going through chemotherapy and didn't feel like eating, I could still enjoy this refreshing juice. It was a real blessing for me—that's why I call it "wonder juice." It's surprisingly delicious and sweet, thanks to the apples. Gala apples are my favorite, but if you can't find them, you can use any sweet apple.

Process the carrots in a juicer and immediately store the remaining pulp in a plastic bag. Freeze the carrot pulp for later use in such recipes as carrot cake or spaghetti sauce. If you use organic carrots, leave the peels on. If the carrots are not organic, peel them before juicing. —Maya

Carrots, 4
Celery, 2 stalks
Spinach leaves, 1 cup
Broccoli florets, ½ cup
Beet, 1 thin slice, peeled
Gala apples, 1 to 2, unpeeled

Prep Time: 10 minutes | **Total Time:** 15 minutes | **1 Serving**

1 In a juicer, combine the carrots, celery, spinach, broccoli, beet, and apples. Process according to machine directions.

2 Drink immediately for best flavor and nutritional value.

Per Serving
Calories, 200
Total fat, 1.2 g
    Saturated fat, 0.2 g
    Trans fat, 0.0 g
    Polyunsaturated fat, 0.5 g
    Monounsaturated fat, 0.1 g
Total carbohydrate, 47 g
    Dietary fiber, 3 g
    Sugars, 28 g
Protein, 5 g
Sodium, 275 mg

papaya and almond smoothie

Nonfat plain or vanilla yogurt, 1 cup

Papaya, chopped, 1 cup

Strawberries, fresh or frozen, chopped, ⅓ cup

Milk (skim or 1 percent), 1 cup

Vanilla extract, 1 teaspoon

Honey or agave nectar, 2 tablespoons, optional

Slivered almonds, 2 tablespoons

Chopped almonds, 2 tablespoons, optional

You can use peaches or melon if you don't have papaya on hand for this smoothie. You can also use whole almonds instead of slivered almonds— just blend them a little longer. Almonds give smoothies a delicious taste and are very nutritious. —Martin

Prep Time: 5 minutes | **Total Time:** 5 minutes | **4 Servings** (about 1 cup each)

1 Combine the yogurt, papaya, strawberries, milk, vanilla, honey, and almonds in a blender and mix well. Sprinkle chopped almonds on each serving, if desired.

Per Serving
Calories, 126
Total fat, 2.2 g
    Saturated fat, 0.3 g
    Trans fat, 0.0 g
    Polyunsaturated fat, 0.5 g
    Monounsaturated fat, 1.3 g
Total carbohydrate, 21 g
    Dietary fiber, 1 g
    Sugars, 19 g
Protein, 6 g
Sodium, 68 mg

frozen fruit smoothie

Milk (skim or 1 percent), 2 cups

Mango, 4 slices

Strawberries, 6, hulled

Raspberries, blueberries, or blackberries, ⅓ cup

Nonfat vanilla frozen yogurt, ½ cup

Honey or brown sugar, 2 tablespoons, optional

The fruit can, of course, be fresh, but using frozen fruit makes it a snap to prepare any time. Other seasonal fruits can be used in this recipe, such as peaches, bananas, pineapple, cantaloupe, or any combination of fresh or frozen berries. We love making this fun recipe with our kids. —Malena and Maya

Prep Time: 5 minutes | **Total Time:** 10 minutes | **4 Servings**

1 Combine all the ingredients in a blender and mix until the fruits are completely puréed. Serve immediately.

Per Serving
Calories, 100
Total fat, 0.3 g
    Saturated fat, 0.1 g
    Trans fat, 0.0 g
    Polyunsaturated fat, 0.1 g
    Monounsaturated fat, 0.1 g
Total carbohydrate, 20 g
    Dietary fiber, 2 g
    Sugars, 17 g
Protein, 6 g
Sodium, 69 mg

American Cancer Society

quinoa and apple smoothie booster

This smoothie supplement adds delicious flavor and rich nutrients to any fruit smoothie. I like to prepare it ahead of time and keep it in the refrigerator. When I'm making a smoothie, I add about ⅓ to ½ cup of this supplement to the blender for a great, complete breakfast.

Quinoa is a complete protein and is considered by many to be a super grain. It is wheat-free and easy to digest, so it is ideal for those who require a gluten-free diet. For the best flavor, I use the original quinoa and not the "quick cooking" variety. —Maya

Quinoa, uncooked, ½ cup

Water, 1½ cups, divided

Cinnamon, 1 small stick

Granny Smith apples, 3, peeled, cored, and finely chopped

Sugar, 1 tablespoon

Milk (2 percent), 1 cup, warmed

Agave nectar or honey, 3 tablespoons

Almonds, finely chopped, ¼ cup

Vanilla extract, ½ teaspoon

Salt, pinch

Prep Time: 20 minutes | **Total Time:** 30 to 45 minutes | **6 Servings**

1 Wash the quinoa in a large bowl of fresh water, rubbing the grains with your fingers. Drain the quinoa by using a fine mesh colander and rinse again by using fresh water. Wash the quinoa four to five times, until no foam appears.

2 Bring 1 cup of water to a boil. Add the quinoa and cinnamon stick and cook for 1 minute. Stir, cover, and reduce heat to low. Let cook for about 15 minutes, or until the grains burst and look like half moons and the water has been absorbed. Remove the cinnamon stick.

3 While the quinoa is cooking, combine the chopped apples, ½ cup water, and the sugar in a small saucepan. Cover and bring to a boil. Reduce heat and cook for 10 minutes, or until the apples are soft.

4 Once the apples soften, remove from the heat. Transfer to a food processor or blender and purée. Add the quinoa and warm milk and blend well.

5 Transfer the apple and quinoa mixture to a bowl. Add the agave nectar, almonds, vanilla, and a pinch of salt. Mix well.

6 Keep the mixture refrigerated until ready to use. This mixture can keep refrigerated for two to three days.

Per Serving
Calories, 158
Total fat, 3.6 g
    Saturated fat, 0.8 g
    Trans fat, 0.0 g
    Polyunsaturated fat, 1.1 g
    Monounsaturated fat, 1.7 g
Total carbohydrate, 28 g
    Dietary fiber, 3 g
    Sugars, 17 g
Protein, 4 g
Sodium, 29 mg

for
children

creamy fruit popsicles

Light cream cheese, 4 ounces

Milk (skim), 2 cups

Pineapple, 5 slices, divided

Peach or apricot, 1, peeled, pitted, and chopped

Honey, 2 tablespoons

Sweetened shredded coconut, 2 tablespoons

These Popsicles can also be made with fresh or frozen berries. Just omit the peach or apricot and add ½ cup of berries to the blender in the first step. —Malena

Prep Time: 10 minutes | **Total Time:** 5 hours | **8 Servings** (one Popsicle each)

1 Combine the cream cheese, milk, three slices of the pineapple, the peach, and honey in a blender and blend well.

2 Finely chop the two remaining pineapple slices and add to the blender. Blend lightly to somewhat break down the pineapple, but do not blend completely.

3 Add the shredded coconut and process gently. Do not blend completely.

4 Pour the mixture into plastic Popsicle molds and freeze for about 5 hours.

Per Serving
Calories, 102
Total fat, 3.7 g
    Saturated fat, 2.2 g
    Trans fat, 0.0 g
    Polyunsaturated fat, 0.2 g
    Monounsaturated fat, 0.9 g
Total carbohydrate, 15 g
    Dietary fiber, 1 g
    Sugars, 13 g
Protein, 4 g
Sodium, 90 mg

salmon cakes

Serve these delicious cakes hot with a side of applesauce, either homemade or store-bought. Kids will love this sweet and savory combination. When my children were small, they often requested it!
—Maya

Pink salmon packed in water, 1 (15-ounce) can

Soda or saltine crackers, 6 to 8, crushed

Eggs, 2

Dried parsley, 1 teaspoon

Salt and ground black pepper, to taste

Prep Time: 15 minutes | **Total Time:** 30 minutes | **6 Servings** (one medium-sized cake each)

1. Drain the salmon, reserving the water. Place the drained salmon in a bowl and crush into small pieces with a fork, removing the large bones.

2. Add the crushed crackers, eggs, parsley, salt, and pepper and mix thoroughly. If the mixture is too dry, add the drained salmon water a little at a time, adding no more than 4 tablespoons. Do not let the mixture get too thin or it will not hold together.

3. Using your hands, form medium-sized balls and flatten into small cakes.

4. Coat a frying pan with nonstick cooking spray and fry half the cakes until golden brown. Press the cakes down with a spatula while they are cooking.

5. Remove the cakes from the frying pan to a paper towel-lined plate. Add more cooking spray if needed and repeat this process for the second batch.

Per Serving
Calories, 128
Total fat, 5.4 g
    Saturated fat, 1.2 g
    Trans fat, 0.0 g
    Polyunsaturated fat, 1.5 g
    Monounsaturated fat, 1.5 g
Total carbohydrate, 2 g
    Dietary fiber, 0 g
    Sugars, 0 g
Protein, 16 g
Sodium, 344 mg

zesty watermelon

This is a great recipe for parties and family gatherings during the summer. Other seasonal fruits can be used in place of watermelon, such as peaches, other melons, papaya, or any combination of berries. For younger children, you can omit the chili powder or use less. —Maya

Watermelon, cubed, 4 cups, chilled

Chili powder, 1 teaspoon

Salt, to taste

Limes, 3, divided

Prep Time: 5 minutes | **Total Time:** 5 minutes | **4 Servings**

1 Place the chilled watermelon into individual glasses or glass bowls.

2 Mix the chili powder and a pinch of salt together. It is best to put the mixture in a salt shaker to better control the amount of spice being sprinkled onto the watermelon.

3 Juice two limes. Sprinkle the watermelon with lime juice and the chili powder mixture, according to the child's preference.

4 Cut the remaining lime into wedges and serve with the watermelon.

Per Serving
Calories, 49
Total fat, 0.4 g
  Saturated fat, 0.0 g
  Trans fat, 0.0 g
  Polyunsaturated fat, 0.1 g
  Monounsaturated fat, 0.1 g
Total carbohydrate, 12 g
  Dietary fiber, 1 g
  Sugars, 10 g
Protein, 1 g
Sodium, 9 mg

rainbow yogurt

Granola, ½ cup

Raisins, 3 tablespoons

Honey, 2 tablespoons

Mango, 1, peeled, pitted, and cubed

Strawberries, 8, hulled and chopped

Blueberries, ½ cup

Nonfat plain or vanilla yogurt, 2 cups

This recipe would also be good with other seasonal fruits, such as peaches, bananas, or any combination of fresh or frozen berries.
—Maya

Prep Time: 15 minutes | **Total Time:** 15 minutes | **4 Servings**

---

1 Combine the granola, raisins, and honey in a small bowl. Set aside.

2 Combine the mango, strawberries, and blueberries in a separate bowl.

3 Cover the bottom of each serving glass with a layer of the fruit mixture.

4 Add a layer of yogurt and top with another layer of fruit.

5 Sprinkle a few tablespoons of the granola and raisin mixture on top. Garnish with strawberries or other fruit if desired.

Per Serving
Calories, 233
Total fat, 3.0 g
  Saturated fat, 0.4 g
  Trans fat, 0.0 g
  Polyunsaturated fat, 0.5 g
  Monounsaturated fat, 0.7 g
Total carbohydrate, 46 g
  Dietary fiber, 3 g
  Sugars, 35 g
Protein, 8 g
Sodium, 84 mg

fruit and yogurt pops

These Popsicles are an easy and healthy treat. Use whatever seasonal fruits you can find, such as peaches, pineapple, mango, papaya, or any kind of fresh or frozen berries. This is a fun recipe to make with kids.
—Maya

Any fruit, coarsely chopped, 2 cups
Low-fat vanilla Greek yogurt, 1 cup
Honey, 1 tablespoon, optional
Almond extract, ½ teaspoon, optional

Prep Time: 5 minutes | **Total Time:** 4 hours | **4 Servings** (one Popsicle each)

---

1 Put all the ingredients in a blender and process until smooth.

2 Pour the mixture into plastic Popsicle molds and freeze for 4 hours.

Per Serving
Calories, 71
Total fat, 0.2 g
    Saturated fat, 0.0 g
    Trans fat, 0.0 g
    Polyunsaturated fat, 0.0 g
    Monounsaturated fat, 0.0 g
Total carbohydrate, 12 g
    Dietary fiber, 1 g
    Sugars, 10 g
Protein, 6 g
Sodium, 24 mg

tortilla chip salad

Boneless, skinless chicken breasts, 2

Limes, 3, divided

Taco seasoning, 1 tablespoon

Salt, ¼ teaspoon

Ground black pepper, ¼ teaspoon

Canola or olive oil, 1 tablespoon

Onion, ½, coarsely chopped

Garlic, 1 clove, chopped

Tomatoes, 2, diced

Lettuce, ½ head, chopped

Frozen corn, 1 cup, thawed, or 1 (8.5-ounce) can whole kernel corn, drained

Black beans, 1 (15-ounce) can, drained and rinsed

Reduced-fat Cheddar cheese, shredded, 1 cup

Classic Pico de Gallo (page 30) or store-bought salsa, 1 cup

Reduced-fat sour cream or Mexican crema, ½ cup

Corn tortilla chips, crumbled, 1 cup

This is one of my kids' favorite recipes and a great way to get children to eat salad. Mexican crema can be found at any Hispanic market.
—Malena

Prep Time: 20 minutes | **Total Time:** 30 minutes | **6 Servings**

1 Season the chicken with the juice of one lime, the taco seasoning, and the salt and pepper.

2 Heat the canola oil in a frying pan and sauté the onion until it is translucent. Add the garlic and cook for 1 to 2 minutes.

3 Add the chicken and cook, covered, over medium-high heat until golden brown and cooked through, about 10 minutes. Remove from heat and shred or cut into bite-sized pieces.

4 In a large glass bowl or casserole dish, arrange all the ingredients in layers, starting with the shredded chicken and continuing with tomatoes, lettuce, corn, black beans, cheese, salsa, and sour cream. Top with crumbled tortilla chips. Cut the remaining two limes into wedges and serve alongside the salad.

Per Serving
Calories, 303
Total fat, 12.2 g
  Saturated fat, 4.6 g
  Trans fat, 0.0 g
  Polyunsaturated fat, 2.2 g
  Monounsaturated fat, 4.4 g
Total carbohydrate, 29 g
  Dietary fiber, 6 g
  Sugars, 7 g
Protein, 22 g
Sodium, 466 mg

special pesto pasta

Bowtie pasta or other small pasta, 10 ounces

Spinach leaves, 2 cups

Fresh basil leaves, ¼ cup

Pine nuts or walnuts, ⅓ cup

Garlic, 1 clove

Olive oil, ⅓ cup

Parmesan cheese, shredded, ½ cup

Salt and ground black pepper, to taste

For an added splash of color and flavor, garnish this dish with cherry tomatoes or any kind of sliced tomatoes. Kids love this dish, and they have no idea they are eating spinach! The pesto can also be served with vegetables or crackers, as an appetizer. —Malena and Maya

Prep Time: 15 minutes | **Total Time:** 25 minutes | **6 Servings**

1 Cook the pasta according to the instructions on the package. When ready, drain and set aside.

2 While the pasta is cooking, wash the spinach and basil thoroughly and dry.

3 In a food processor, combine the spinach, basil, and pine nuts. Begin to blend. Add the clove of garlic and continue blending.

4 With the motor running, gradually add the olive oil. When the ingredients are blended, add the cheese and continue blending until the mixture is uniform. Season with salt and pepper, to taste.

5 Combine the pesto sauce and pasta. Mix and serve.

Per Serving
Calories, 367
Total fat, 20.3 g
    Saturated fat, 3.5 g
    Trans fat, 0.0 g
    Polyunsaturated fat, 4.4 g
    Monounsaturated fat, 11.0 g
Total carbohydrate, 37 g
    Dietary fiber, 2 g
    Sugars, 3 g
Protein, 10 g
Sodium, 69 mg

yolita's mashed potatoes

I think of this recipe with delight. When my sisters and I were children, our mother would serve the potatoes in the shape of a sun with potato "rays" all around. Sometimes she made a face on the potatoes with cooked vegetables. Little did we know, she was trying to pack as many nutrients as possible into our meals! —Maya

Potatoes, 6 large

Sweet potato or yam, 1, quartered

Carrots, 1 to 2, chopped

Butter, 3 tablespoons, divided

Canned cooked pumpkin, 1 cup, or 1 (14-ounce) bag frozen pumpkin, thawed

Kosher salt, to taste

Milk (skim), 1 cup plus 2 tablespoons, warmed, divided

Prep Time: 20 minutes | **Total Time:** 45 minutes to 1 hour | **6 Servings**

1 Peel and cut each potato into four to six pieces. Place in a pot with water to cover and bring to a boil. Cook until potatoes are soft. Drain well.

2 Meanwhile, fill a separate pan with water and bring to a boil. Add the sweet potato and carrots and cook until soft. Drain well.

3 Melt 1 tablespoon of the butter in a pan. Lightly sauté the cooked pumpkin. Add the sweet potato and carrots with a pinch of salt and cook for 10 minutes.

4 Place the pumpkin, sweet potato, and carrots in a blender with 2 tablespoons of the milk and blend thoroughly, making sure the mix doesn't get too runny. Set aside.

5 When the potatoes are cooked, drain the water and mash them. Add the remaining 2 tablespoons of butter and ½ cup of the warm milk. Beat with an electric hand mixer until creamy.

6 Add the remaining ½ cup of warm milk and the pumpkin mixture to the mashed potatoes. If you want a marbleized, two-color appearance, lightly fold the vegetable mixture into the potatoes with a spoon or spatula. Otherwise, mix well with the hand mixer. Taste and adjust seasoning as necessary.

Per Serving
Calories, 255
Total fat, 6.1 g
    Saturated fat, 3.8 g
    Trans fat, 0.2 g
    Polyunsaturated fat, 0.3 g
    Monounsaturated fat, 1.5 g
Total carbohydrate, 46 g
    Dietary fiber, 5 g
    Sugars, 7 g
Protein, 6 g
Sodium, 96 mg

veggie tortilla pizza

This is an easy recipe that kids will love to help prepare. These pizzas can also be made with sliced olives, other vegetables, or other herbs or spices. —Maya

Prep Time: 10 minutes | **Total Time:** 20 minutes | **8 Servings**

1 Preheat oven to 350 degrees.

2 Place the tortillas on baking sheets. Spread 2 tablespoons of pizza sauce on each tortilla. Rub the oregano between your fingers and sprinkle over the tortillas.

3 Add onion to each tortilla and then spread out the peppers and pineapple.

4 Sprinkle with mozzarella cheese and Parmesan cheese.

5 Bake for 10 minutes or until the cheese melts.

Whole wheat tortillas (8-inch), 8

Pizza sauce, 1 cup

Dried oregano, 1 teaspoon

Red onion, ½, finely chopped

Red bell pepper, 1, stemmed, seeded, and cut into strips

Green bell pepper, 1, stemmed, seeded, and cut into strips

Pineapple tidbits in 100 percent juice, 1 (8-ounce) can, drained

Reduced-fat mozzarella cheese, shredded, 1 cup

Parmesan cheese, grated, 2 to 3 tablespoons

Rubbing the oregano between your fingers will help to release its flavor.

Per Serving
Calories, 249
Total fat, 7.6 g
    Saturated fat, 3.9 g
    Trans fat, 0.0 g
    Polyunsaturated fat, 1.4 g
    Monounsaturated fat, 1.1 g
Total carbohydrate, 36 g
    Dietary fiber, 5 g
    Sugars, 7 g
Protein, 10 g
Sodium, 723 mg

mexican mini pizzas

Reduced-fat mozzarella cheese, shredded, 1 cup

Corn tortillas, 16

Tomato sauce, 1 cup

Green bell pepper, 1, stemmed, seeded, and finely chopped

Red bell pepper, 1, stemmed, seeded, and finely chopped

Yellow bell pepper, 1, stemmed, seeded, and finely chopped

Honey-cured ham, 4 slices, coarsely chopped, optional

Panela cheese, shredded, ½ cup

Crushed red pepper, optional

Kids and adults love pizza, and this recipe is an easy and healthy way to prepare it at home. Kids can help put the pizzas together, once you've chopped the ingredients. Panela cheese can be found in the cheese section of many supermarkets, not just in Hispanic markets. —Martín

Prep Time: 15 minutes | **Total Time:** 25 minutes | **8 Servings**

1 Preheat oven to 380 degrees.

2 Sprinkle mozzarella cheese on top of eight tortillas. Cover them with the remaining tortillas.

3 Cook the tortillas in a frying pan or on a griddle over medium heat just until the cheese melts.

4 Transfer the tortillas to a baking sheet lined with aluminum foil.

5 Brush tomato sauce on each tortilla. Add the bell peppers and ham and sprinkle with Panela cheese. Sprinkle the crushed red pepper over the pizzas.

6 Bake for 10 minutes, or until the cheese starts to brown. Serve hot.

Per Serving
Calories, 187
Total fat, 6.0 g
    Saturated fat, 3.0 g
    Trans fat, 0.0 g
    Polyunsaturated fat, 1.0 g
    Monounsaturated fat, 1.3 g
Total carbohydrate, 27 g
    Dietary fiber, 4 g
    Sugars, 4 g
Protein, 9 g
Sodium, 286 mg

mashed potatoes with spinach

My mother prepared this recipe for my sisters and me when we were little. She would sprinkle the green mashed potatoes with small flowers cut out of cooked carrots and beets. My sisters and I were always delighted to eat our "beautiful green prairies sprinkled with flowers." We never even realized we were eating spinach! What a wise woman my mother was! Maybe she will inspire you to do the same for your children. —Maya

Potatoes, 6 large

Unsalted butter, 3 tablespoons, divided

Fresh spinach, 2 cups, or 1 (10-ounce) package frozen spinach, thawed and drained well

Kosher salt, to taste

Milk (skim), 1 cup plus 2 tablespoons, warmed, divided

Prep Time: 10 minutes | **Total Time:** 45 minutes | **6 Servings**

1 Peel and cut each potato into four to six pieces and put into a pot. Add water until potatoes are fully covered. Bring to a boil and cook until potatoes are soft.

2 Heat 1 tablespoon of the butter in a pan. Add the spinach and a pinch of salt and sauté for 3 to 5 minutes, until reduced. If using frozen spinach, cook until heated through and fragrant, several minutes. Once the spinach has reduced, place it in a blender with 2 tablespoons of the milk and blend thoroughly, making sure it doesn't get too runny. Set aside.

3 When the potatoes are cooked, drain and mash them. Add the remaining 2 tablespoons of butter and ½ cup of the warm milk. Beat with an electric hand mixer until creamy.

4 Add the blended spinach and the remaining ½ cup of warm milk to the potatoes. If you want a marbleized, two-color appearance, lightly fold the spinach into the mashed potatoes with a spoon or spatula. Otherwise, mix well with the hand mixer. Taste and adjust seasoning as needed.

Per Serving
Calories, 219
Total fat, 6.0 g
    Saturated fat, 3.7 g
    Trans fat, 0.2 g
    Polyunsaturated fat, 0.3 g
    Monounsaturated fat, 1.5 g
Total carbohydrate, 38 g
    Dietary fiber, 3 g
    Sugars, 4 g
Protein, 5 g
Sodium, 87 mg

salads

classic vinaigrette

Freshly squeezed lime or lemon juice, 2 tablespoons

Salt and ground black pepper, to taste

Extra-virgin olive oil, ¼ cup

Garlic, 1 clove

Eat a salad every day! With homemade salad dressings, any salad can be especially delicious. Homemade salad dressings are incredibly easy to make and much better for you than store-bought dressings. They're also more economical! You can throw anything into your salad—I like to start with the basics: lettuce (with dark leaves), tomatoes of some sort, shredded carrots, and cucumber. I add avocado to almost all my salads. You can add fruit, if you like. Just use your imagination!

The secret to enhancing the flavor of this dressing (and the recipe that follows) is to crush the garlic as the final step and immediately add it to the dressing. This dressing will keep for at least three to four days, refrigerated. —Malena

Prep Time: 10 minutes | **Total Time:** 10 minutes | **Makes about ⅓ cup**

1 Place the lime juice, salt, and pepper in a glass bowl and mix.

2 Add the oil gradually, whisking or stirring briskly with a fork to blend the ingredients thoroughly.

3 Finally, peel and crush the garlic clove and add it to the dressing. The garlic can also be minced. Set aside for a few minutes before serving.

Per Serving (about 1 tablespoon)
Calories, 81
Total fat, 9.0 g
    Saturated fat, 1.2 g
    Trans fat, 0.0 g
    Polyunsaturated fat, 1.0 g
    Monounsaturated fat, 6.6 g
Total carbohydrate, 0 g
    Dietary fiber, 0 g
    Sugars, 0 g
Protein, 0 g
Sodium, 1 mg

classic mustard vinaigrette

This is a fancier but still easy salad dressing that can also be used as a sauce for cooked vegetables, such as beets, steamed broccoli, or Brussels sprouts. This dressing will keep for at least three to four days, refrigerated. —Malena

Red wine vinegar, 2 tablespoons
Dijon mustard, ½ teaspoon
Salt and ground black pepper, to taste
Extra-virgin olive oil, ¼ cup
Garlic, 1 clove

Prep Time: 10 minutes | **Total Time:** 10 minutes | **Makes about ⅓ cup**

1 Place the red wine vinegar, mustard, salt, and pepper in a glass bowl and mix.

2 Add the oil gradually, whisking or stirring briskly with a fork to blend the ingredients thoroughly.

3 Finally, peel and crush the garlic clove and add to the dressing. Set aside for a few minutes before serving.

Per Serving (about 1 tablespoon)
Calories, 82
Total fat, 9.0 g
    Saturated fat, 1.2 g
    Trans fat, 0.0 g
    Polyunsaturated fat, 1.0 g
    Monounsaturated fat, 6.6 g
Total carbohydrate, 0 g
    Dietary fiber, 0 g
    Sugars, 0 g
Protein, 0 g
Sodium, 11 mg

homemade ranch dressing

Reduced-fat buttermilk, 1 cup

Reduced-fat mayonnaise, ⅔ cup

Reduced-fat sour cream, ⅔ cup

Garlic powder, 1 teaspoon

Onion powder, 1 teaspoon

Fresh chives, chopped, 2 teaspoons

Fresh dill, chopped, 2 teaspoons

Fresh flat leaf parsley or cilantro leaves, chopped, 2 teaspoons

Salt and ground black pepper, to taste

My friend Glenda Sellar gave me the recipe for this delectable ranch dressing. If you can find fresh herbs, they make the dressing even better. Dried will be almost as good—just use a little less. This dressing will keep refrigerated for a couple of days. —Malena

Prep Time: 10 minutes | **Total Time:** 45 minutes, including refrigeration | **Makes about 2½ cups**

1 Whisk together the buttermilk, mayonnaise, and sour cream in a bowl.

2 Add the garlic powder, onion powder, chives, dill, parsley, salt, and pepper. Stir thoroughly.

3 Cover and refrigerate for at least 30 minutes before serving.

Per Serving (about ¼ cup)
Calories, 89
Total fat, 7.2 g
　　Saturated fat, 2.2 g
　　Trans fat, 0.0 g
　　Polyunsaturated fat, 3.0 g
　　Monounsaturated fat, 1.7 g
Total carbohydrate, 4 g
　　Dietary fiber, 0 g
　　Sugars, 3 g
Protein, 2 g
Sodium, 177 mg

raspberry dressing

I love this salad dressing because it is rich and delicate at the same time, thanks to the raspberries. This dressing can be stored for two to three days in the refrigerator. It makes any salad elegant and delicious. —Maya

Prep Time: 5 minutes | **Total Time:** 40 minutes, including refrigeration | **Makes about 2 cups**

1 Put the raspberries in a blender with ⅓ cup water and purée. Strain in a mesh sieve to separate the seeds. Set aside.

2 Put the olive oil, half-and-half, vinegar, honey, salt, and black and white pepper in the blender and mix well.

3 Add the raspberry purée to the blender and mix well for a couple of minutes.

4 Refrigerate for 30 minutes and serve.

Raspberries, fresh or frozen, 1 cup

Water, ⅓ cup

Extra-virgin olive oil, ⅓ cup

Low-fat half-and-half or evaporated milk, ¼ cup

White wine vinegar, 2 tablespoons

Honey or agave nectar, 2 to 3 tablespoons

Salt, ¼ teaspoon

Ground black pepper, ⅛ teaspoon

Ground white pepper, ⅛ teaspoon

Per Serving (about ¼ cup)
Calories, 111
Total fat, 9.5 g
    Saturated fat, 1.5 g
    Trans fat, 0.0 g
    Polyunsaturated fat, 1.0 g
    Monounsaturated fat, 6.7 g
Total carbohydrate, 7 g
    Dietary fiber, 0 g
    Sugars, 5 g
Protein, 0 g
Sodium, 81 mg

honey mustard vinaigrette

Dijon mustard, 2 tablespoons

Honey or agave nectar, 3 tablespoons

Balsamic vinegar, ¼ cup

Extra-virgin olive oil, ¼ cup

Canola oil, ½ cup

Salt, ½ teaspoon, or to taste

Ground black pepper, ¼ teaspoon, or to taste

Boiling water, ¼ cup

Everyone in my family loves this vinaigrette. I love it because it gets my family to eat salads! Since this vinaigrette is very thick, it can also be used as a dip for veggies, such as cherry tomatoes, raw or cooked broccoli, cauliflower, mushrooms, carrots, or jicama. This vinaigrette also makes a delicious marinade for meat, chicken, or fish. —Maya

Prep Time: 5 minutes | **Total Time:** 10 minutes | **12 Servings** (about 2 tablespoons each)

1 Place all the ingredients in a blender and blend thoroughly.

2 Taste and adjust seasoning as desired. Serve immediately.

Per Serving
Calories, 143
Total fat, 13.7 g
    Saturated fat, 1.3 g
    Trans fat, 0.0 g
    Polyunsaturated fat, 3.0 g
    Monounsaturated fat, 9.1 g
Total carbohydrate, 6 g
    Dietary fiber, 0 g
    Sugars, 5 g
Protein, 0 g
Sodium, 159 mg

salad dressing for jicama and avocado

Jicama is a vegetable native to Mexico. Shaped like a large onion, it has a thick, light brown skin and crisp white flesh. It is eaten raw. Its flavor resembles a combination of a crunchy apple or pear and a radish. It is easy to find at Hispanic markets and is becoming easier to find in regular supermarkets. Do not refrigerate it, as it needs to stay dry. Peel and cut into slices or strips to eat. I like to serve julienned jicama with this delectable salad dressing, topped with cubed avocado. This dressing is also delicious on a green salad. —Malena

Red onion, ½, julienned

Freshly squeezed lime juice, 2 tablespoons

Red wine vinegar, 1 tablespoon

Cilantro leaves, finely chopped, 1 tablespoon

Salt, ¼ teaspoon

Ground black pepper, ⅛ teaspoon

Prep Time: 10 minutes | **Total Time:** 40 minutes | **4 Servings** (about 2 tablespoons each)

1 Combine all the ingredients in a glass bowl. Mix well. Let the flavors meld for about 30 minutes.

Per Serving
Calories, 10
Total fat, 0.0 g
    Saturated fat, 0.0 g
    Trans fat, 0.0 g
    Polyunsaturated fat, 0.0 g
    Monounsaturated fat, 0.0 g
Total carbohydrate, 2 g
    Dietary fiber, 0 g
    Sugars, 1 g
Protein, 0 g
Sodium, 148 mg

delicious broccoli salad

Reduced-fat mayonnaise, ¼ cup

Honey, 1 tablespoon

Apple cider vinegar, 1 tablespoon

Broccoli florets, 2 cups, uncooked

Raisins, ¼ cup

Walnuts, chopped, ¼ cup

Roasted, salted sesame seeds, 2 teaspoons, optional

Each time I prepare this salad for a party, it's the first dish that goes; many people ask me for the recipe. This recipe is a delicious way to enjoy broccoli, a nutrition powerhouse. —Maya

Prep Time: 10 minutes | **Total Time:** 10 minutes | **6 Servings**

1 In a glass bowl, combine the mayonnaise, honey, and vinegar. Mix thoroughly.

2 Add the broccoli, raisins, and walnuts and mix well.

3 Before serving, sprinkle with the sesame seeds.

Per Serving
Calories, 101
Total fat, 6.7 g
    Saturated fat, 0.8 g
    Trans fat, 0.0 g
    Polyunsaturated fat, 4.2 g
    Monounsaturated fat, 1.3 g
Total carbohydrate, 10 g
    Dietary fiber, 1 g
    Sugars, 8 g
Protein, 2 g
Sodium, 93 mg

apple, celery, and avocado salad

My mother makes this salad during the summer, and the whole family loves it. —Martín

Prep Time: 20 minutes | **Total Time:** 45 minutes | **6 Servings**

1 In a small bowl, cover the raisins with the red wine. In separate bowls, cover the celery with cold water and the apples with salted cold water or freshly squeezed lime juice. Let all sit for 30 minutes. Drain well and set aside.

2 In the meantime, place the almonds in an ungreased skillet over medium heat. Cook, stirring frequently, for 5 to 7 minutes, until the almonds are lightly browned. Be careful not to let them burn.

3 Combine the raisins, celery, apples, almonds, avocado, lime juice, yogurt, and mayonnaise in a large bowl. Mix thoroughly and sprinkle with pepper. Serve immediately.

Raisins, ½ cup

Red wine, ½ cup

Celery, 4 stalks, chopped

Granny Smith apples, 3, cored and cubed

Sliced or slivered almonds, ½ cup

Avocado, 1, peeled, pitted, and cubed

Freshly squeezed lime juice, 1 teaspoon

Nonfat plain or vanilla Greek yogurt, ½ cup

Reduced-fat mayonnaise, ¼ cup

Ground black pepper, ¼ teaspoon, or to taste

Soaking the apples in saltwater or lime juice will prevent them from turning brown.

Per Serving
Calories, 205
Total fat, 10.9 g
  Saturated fat, 1.4 g
  Trans fat, 0.0 g
  Polyunsaturated fat, 3.2 g
  Monounsaturated fat, 5.6 g
Total carbohydrate, 26 g
  Dietary fiber, 5 g
  Sugars, 17 g
Protein, 5 g
Sodium, 139 mg

red bell pepper and orange salad

Romaine lettuce, 1 head, cut into long, thin strips

Oranges, 3, peeled and segmented

Red bell peppers, 2, stemmed, seeded, and cut into thin strips

Walnut halves, ½ cup

Extra-virgin olive oil, ½ cup

Dijon mustard, 2 tablespoons

Honey, 2 tablespoons

Freshly squeezed orange juice, 2 tablespoons

Salt and ground black pepper, to taste

To reduce calories in this recipe, serve the dressing on the side. Pour just a spoonful of dressing onto the salad immediately before eating. —Malena

Prep Time: 20 minutes | **Total Time:** 20 minutes | **8 Servings**

1 Place the lettuce, orange segments, red pepper, and walnuts into a salad bowl and mix thoroughly.

2 To prepare the dressing, combine the oil, mustard, honey, orange juice, and salt and pepper. Mix well.

3 To serve, dress each portion of salad with a spoonful of dressing and toss.

Per Serving
Calories, 226
Total fat, 18.0 g
    Saturated fat, 2.3 g
    Trans fat, 0.0 g
    Polyunsaturated fat, 4.5 g
    Monounsaturated fat, 10.5 g
Total carbohydrate, 17 g
    Dietary fiber, 4 g
    Sugars, 13 g
Protein, 3 g
Sodium, 95 mg

pear and blue cheese salad

Romaine lettuce, 1 head, or 1 (6-ounce) package lettuce, mixed greens, or romaine, cut or torn into pieces

Oranges, 2, or 4 mandarin oranges, peeled and segmented

Pears, 2, peeled, cored, and cubed

Walnuts, coarsely chopped, ½ cup

Blue cheese, crumbled, 2 ounces (about ½ cup)

Dried cranberries, ¼ cup

Freshly squeezed orange juice, ¼ cup

Extra-virgin olive oil, 1 tablespoon

Salt, to taste

This refreshing salad is great for parties. The combination of blue cheese and pears is delicious. —Martín

Prep Time: 25 minutes | **Total Time:** 25 minutes | **8 Servings**

1 Rinse the lettuce in cold water and dry with a paper towel. Place in a large bowl and set aside.

2 In a separate bowl, combine the orange segments, pears, walnuts, blue cheese, and cranberries and toss to mix. Add this mixture to the lettuce.

3 In a glass container, combine the orange juice and olive oil and whisk briskly. Season with salt to taste.

4 To serve, pour the dressing on the salad and mix well.

Per Serving
Calories, 173
Total fat, 9.4 g
   Saturated fat, 2.3 g
   Trans fat, 0.1 g
   Polyunsaturated fat, 3.9 g
   Monounsaturated fat, 2.6 g
Total carbohydrate, 21 g
   Dietary fiber, 4 g
   Sugars, 14 g
Protein, 4 g
Sodium, 122 mg

tomato and cucumber salad

This is an easy, delicious, and nutritious Greek-style salad to make for your family. —Malena

Prep Time: 15 minutes | **Total Time:** 30 minutes | **4 Servings**

1 Combine all the ingredients in a large glass bowl and mix well.

2 Let the flavors meld for 15 minutes. Taste and add salt and pepper as needed before serving.

Roma tomatoes, 4, diced

Cucumbers, 2, peeled and chopped

Green onions, 4, chopped

Juice of 2 limes

Olive oil, 2 tablespoons

Garlic, 2 cloves, minced

Flat leaf parsley, chopped, 2 tablespoons

Salt and ground black pepper, to taste

Per Serving
Calories, 102
Total fat, 7.2 g
    Saturated fat, 1.0 g
    Trans fat, 0.0 g
    Polyunsaturated fat, 0.8 g
    Monounsaturated fat, 5.0 g
Total carbohydrate, 9 g
    Dietary fiber, 3 g
    Sugars, 5 g
Protein, 2 g
Sodium, 13 mg

watercress-mango salad

This refreshing salad is not only delicious and nutritious but also beautiful. —Malena

---

Prep Time: 30 minutes | **Total Time:** 30 minutes | **6 Servings**

---

1 Combine all the ingredients in a large glass bowl. Taste and adjust seasoning and serve.

Watercress, 1 pound, rinsed, stemmed, and coarsely chopped

Spinach, stemmed and coarsely chopped, 1 cup

Mangoes, 2, pitted, peeled, and cubed

Tomato, 1 large, diced

Cucumber, 1, peeled and diced

Red onion, ½, finely chopped

Balsamic vinegar or red wine vinegar, 2 tablespoons

Juice of 1 lemon

Salt and ground black pepper, to taste

Per Serving
Calories, 80
Total fat, 0.4 g
    Saturated fat, 0.1 g
    Trans fat, 0.0 g
    Polyunsaturated fat, 0.1 g
    Monounsaturated fat, 0.1 g
Total carbohydrate, 19 g
    Dietary fiber, 3 g
    Sugars, 14 g
Protein, 3 g
Sodium, 39 mg

apple salad with peanuts and raisins

Apples, 4, peeled, cored, and cubed

Freshly squeezed lime juice, ¼ cup

Orange juice, ¼ cup

Unsalted dry roasted peanuts, ½ cup, chopped

Raisins, ½ cup (about 2 small boxes)

Nonfat vanilla Greek yogurt, 1 cup

Honey, 2 tablespoons, optional

Kids love this salad. Aside from being delicious, it's easy and fun for them to help prepare. —Martín

Prep Time: 15 minutes | **Total Time:** 45 minutes | **8 Servings**

1 Soak the cubed apples in a bowl of saltwater for 30 minutes to prevent them from turning brown. Drain apples and set aside.

2 Combine the lime juice and orange juice in a bowl. Add the apples, peanuts, and raisins. Cover and marinate in the refrigerator for 15 minutes.

3 Drain the apple mixture and place in a salad bowl. Add the yogurt and honey. Mix well.

Per Serving
Calories, 131
Total fat, 5.1 g
    Saturated fat, 0.7 g
    Trans fat, 0.0 g
    Polyunsaturated fat, 1.6 g
    Monounsaturated fat, 2.5 g
Total carbohydrate, 18 g
    Dietary fiber, 2 g
    Sugars, 13 g
Protein, 6 g
Sodium, 19 mg

nopales salad

This recipe comes from Olga V. Fusté's cookbook Cocinando para Latinos con Diabetes (Diabetic Cooking for Latinos), *published by the American Diabetes Association. Nopales are the leaves, or pads, of the prickly pear cactus plant. They are very common in Mexican and Southwestern cooking and have a flavor similar to green beans. If you buy fresh nopales, you will need to remove the thorns before preparing them. Wearing work gloves or holding the paddles with tongs, trim the edges of the leaves and the end where they were connected to the plant. Slice off the needles from both sides of the leaves. You can also peel them with a vegetable peeler.*

You can mix up this recipe in a number of ways—more avocado, less cilantro, a fresh jalapeño for spice, queso fresco instead of Mexican-style cheese—the possibilities are endless. We like to boil the nopales and then sauté them with onion and red pepper before making the salad. It is really a very easy recipe to make your own!

Nopales, 1 pound, fresh or canned

White onion, ½ large, cut into chunks

Salt, ½ teaspoon

Tomatoes, 2 medium, peeled and chopped, or 1 (14-ounce) can chopped tomatoes, drained

Cilantro leaves, finely chopped, ½ cup

Freshly squeezed lime juice, 2 teaspoons

Avocado, ½ medium, peeled, pitted, and cubed

Mexican-style cheese, shredded, ¼ cup

Prep Time: 20 minutes | **Total Time:** 1 hour and 30 minutes | **6 Servings**

1 If using fresh nopales, rinse and pat dry. Cut into ½-inch pieces. If using canned nopales, drain, rinse well, and cut into pieces.

2 Cook nopales in boiling water with onion and salt for 5 minutes. Drain and rinse in cold water. Discard onion.

3 In a medium bowl, combine nopales, tomatoes, cilantro, and lime juice. Refrigerate at least 1 hour. Before serving, add avocado and garnish with cheese. Serve with tortillas.

Per Serving
Calories, 58
Total fat, 3.4 g
    Saturated fat, 1.2 g
    Trans fat, 0.0 g
    Polyunsaturated fat, 0.3 g
    Monounsaturated fat, 1.7 g
Total carbohydrate, 5 g
    Dietary fiber, 3 g
    Sugars, 2 g
Protein, 3 g
Sodium, 97 mg

easy jicama, apple, and carrot salad with lime vinaigrette

Carrots, 3

Jicama, 1 medium

Granny Smith apple, 1

Limes, 3, divided

Tomato, 1 large, cubed

Raisins, ¼ cup

Cilantro leaves, finely chopped, ¼ cup

Canola oil, 1 tablespoon

Garlic, crushed, 1 teaspoon

Cayenne pepper, pinch, optional

Kosher salt, to taste

This refreshing salad makes a delicious accompaniment to grilled chicken or shrimp. If you'd like, you can add a touch of honey at the end. — Maya

Prep Time: 20 minutes | **Total Time:** 20 minutes | **6 Servings**

1 Peel the carrots and jicama. Remove and discard the tough bottom layer of the jicama.

2 Cut the carrots, jicama, and apple into pieces small enough to fit easily into the chute of the food processor. Use the shredding disk to process the carrots, jicama, and apple.

3 Place the shredded carrots, jicama, and apple in a glass bowl. Immediately cover with the juice of one lime to prevent the apple from turning brown. Add the tomato, raisins, and cilantro to the mixture.

4 In a separate small container, combine the canola oil, garlic, the juice of two limes, and cayenne pepper.

5 Pour the dressing over the vegetable mixture. Stir to combine. Add salt to taste and serve.

Per Serving
Calories, 118
Total fat, 2.7 g
    Saturated fat, 0.2 g
    Trans fat, 0.0 g
    Polyunsaturated fat, 0.8 g
    Monounsaturated fat, 1.5 g
Total carbohydrate, 24 g
    Dietary fiber, 8 g
    Sugars, 11 g
Protein, 2 g
Sodium, 31 mg

tarasco's salad

Carrots, coarsely chopped, 1½ cups

Celery, coarsely chopped, 1¼ cups

Onion, chopped, ¼ cup

Sugar, 1 tablespoon

Apple cider vinegar, ½ cup

Canola oil, ¼ cup

Salt, ½ teaspoon

Organic mixed greens with baby spinach and arugula or spring mix lettuce, 1 (10-ounce) package, washed and dried

Granny Smith apples, 2, peeled, cored, and sliced

Peaches, 2, peeled, pitted, and sliced, or 10 strawberries, hulled and sliced

Pecans or walnuts, ½ cup

Parmesan cheese, shredded, to taste

Cotija cheese, crumbled, to taste, optional

This recipe comes from a restaurant in Denver called Tarasco's New Latino Cuisine, owned by Noé Bermúdez. Noé is very proud of serving healthy Mexican dishes in his restaurant. Cotija cheese can be found in Hispanic markets. If you can't locate it, just use the Parmesan cheese.
—Maya

Prep Time: 20 minutes | **Total Time:** 20 minutes | **5 Servings**

1 To prepare the dressing, combine the carrots, celery, onion, sugar, apple cider vinegar, canola oil, and salt in a blender and process thoroughly.

2 Place a handful of mixed greens on each dish and top with the apples, peaches, and pecans. Sprinkle with the cheeses.

3 Add the dressing to the salad immediately before serving. If stored in a lidded glass jar, the dressing should keep for approximately one week, refrigerated.

Per Serving
Calories, 269
Total fat, 19.8 g
    Saturated fat, 1.6 g
    Trans fat, 0.0 g
    Polyunsaturated fat, 5.6 g
    Monounsaturated fat, 11.9 g
Total carbohydrate, 23 g
    Dietary fiber, 5 g
    Sugars, 16 g
Protein, 3 g
Sodium, 297 mg

classic waldorf salad

This classic salad is a delicious accompaniment for roast turkey at Christmas dinner. It brings back fond memories of the exquisite dinners my mom used to make for Christmas in Peru. See the recipe for Roast Turkey on page 136. —Maya

Prep Time: 20 minutes | **Total Time:** 20 minutes | **5 Servings**

1 Put the cubed apples in a bowl and pour the lime juice over them. Toss to coat.

2 Combine all the ingredients except the lettuce leaves in a glass bowl and mix well. Taste and adjust seasoning as needed.

3 Transfer to a serving dish or serve on top of lettuce leaves on individual plates.

Granny Smith apples, 4, peeled, cored, and cubed

Juice of 1 lime

Celery, chopped, ½ cup

Raisins, ¼ cup

Red grapes, ¼ cup, halved

Walnuts, coarsely chopped, ¼ cup

Reduced-fat mayonnaise, ¼ cup

Salt and ground black pepper, to taste

Lettuce leaves, 5 to 6, optional

Per Serving
Calories, 153
Total fat, 8.1 g
   Saturated fat, 1.0 g
   Trans fat, 0.0 g
   Polyunsaturated fat, 5.0 g
   Monounsaturated fat, 1.5 g
Total carbohydrate, 22 g
   Dietary fiber, 2 g
   Sugars, 16 g
Protein, 2 g
Sodium, 113 mg

soups

tlalpeño soup

Onion, chopped, ½ cup

Garlic, 2 cloves

Carrots, 4, sliced

Reduced-sodium chicken broth, 6 cups

Bone-in chicken breasts, 3, skin removed

Epazote, 1 sprig

Garbanzo beans, uncooked, 1 cup, soaked overnight and drained

Salt, to taste

Toppings:

Cilantro leaves, chopped, ¼ cup

Avocado, 1, peeled, pitted, and cubed

Chipotle chili in adobo sauce, chopped, 1 teaspoon

Juice of 1 or 2 limes

This soup is a Mexican classic. It originated in the picturesque area of Tlalpan, in the southern part of Mexico City. It is hearty enough to serve as a one-dish meal and easy to make in a slow cooker. Epazote is an aromatic herb with a distinctive taste that is used in many Mexican dishes. It can be purchased in markets that carry Hispanic produce. If you cannot include epazote in this soup, it will still taste delicious. —Martín

Prep Time: 20 minutes | **Total Time:** 6 to 8 hours | **6 Servings**

1 Coat a frying pan with nonstick cooking spray. Over medium-high heat, add the onion and garlic and sauté for 5 to 7 minutes, or until the onion is translucent.

2 Add the carrots to the onion and garlic and cook, stirring frequently, for 5 to 7 minutes.

3 In the meantime, place the chicken broth and chicken breasts into a slow cooker. Add the fresh epazote and drained garbanzo beans.

4 Add the carrot and onion mixture to the slow cooker and cook for 6 to 8 hours on low.

5 At the end of the cooking time, remove the chicken breasts from the slow cooker and shred or chop the meat. Set aside. Stir the soup to combine. Taste and add salt if necessary. To serve, ladle the soup into bowls and add a portion of chicken. Top with cilantro, cubed avocado, chipotle chili, and freshly squeezed lime juice.

Per Serving
Calories, 294
Total fat, 7.8 g
    Saturated fat, 1.3 g
    Trans fat, 0.0 g
    Polyunsaturated fat, 1.8 g
    Monounsaturated fat, 3.6 g
Total carbohydrate, 28 g
    Dietary fiber, 9 g
    Sugars, 7 g
Protein, 28 g
Sodium, 597 mg

peruvian creamy spinach soup

This soup is excellent for children because they don't even realize they're eating vegetables. My mom made it for our family, and I also make it for mine. It's best not to use much salt because each bowl is served with a sprinkle of Parmesan cheese, which is quite salty. You can also top with croutons if you like. —Maya

White Sauce (page 17), 1 cup

Butter, 2 tablespoons

Canola oil, ½ teaspoon

Garlic, 1 clove, minced

Fresh spinach, 2 pounds, or 2 (8-ounce) packages frozen spinach, thawed and drained

Salt, pinch

Reduced-sodium chicken or vegetable broth, 4 cups, divided

Fat-free evaporated milk, 1 (12-ounce) can

Parmesan cheese, grated, 3 tablespoons

Baked croutons, optional

Prep Time: 20 minutes | **Total Time:** 45 minutes to 1 hour | **6 Servings**

1 In a large, heavy pot, prepare the white sauce that will serve as the base for the soup and set aside.

2 In a separate pot or skillet, heat 2 tablespoons of butter along with the oil to prevent it from burning. Add the garlic, spinach, and a pinch of salt. Lightly sauté until the spinach has wilted. (If using frozen spinach, cook until heated through and fragrant, several minutes.) Working in batches, transfer the cooked spinach to a blender and purée with 1 to 2 cups of broth.

3 Add the blended spinach, the remaining broth, and the evaporated milk to the prepared white sauce. Mix thoroughly and cook for approximately 5 minutes over medium heat.

4 To serve, ladle into individual bowls. Top with Parmesan cheese and croutons.

Per Serving
Calories, 200
Total fat, 10.4 g
    Saturated fat, 6.1 g
    Trans fat, 0.3 g
    Polyunsaturated fat, 0.7 g
    Monounsaturated fat, 3.0 g
Total carbohydrate, 16 g
    Dietary fiber, 3 g
    Sugars, 10 g
Protein, 12 g
Sodium, 803 mg

quick pozole

This hearty soup is great for casual parties with friends and family. It is fun to serve it in traditional Mexican clay bowls and let your guests enjoy adding condiments on top. —Malena and Martín

Prep Time: 15 minutes | **Total Time:** 45 minutes to 1 hour | **8 Servings**

1 Place the chicken in a pot with the chicken broth. Bring to a boil and cook for 10 minutes, or until the chicken is cooked. Remove the chicken, let cool, and shred. Reserve the broth.

2 In a large pan over medium heat, sauté the onion and the garlic in canola oil for 3 minutes. Add the hominy to the pan with the garlic and onion and cook over medium heat for 5 minutes, stirring frequently. Add the shredded chicken to the hominy mixture.

3 In a dry skillet, roast the tomatoes over medium heat, turning to cook on all sides, for 10 minutes, or until peels are soft and darkened.

4 In a blender or food processor, blend the roasted tomatoes, the chipotle chili, and the chili powder with a cup of the reserved chicken broth until smooth.

5 Add the tomato mixture and the rest of the broth to the pan with the chicken and hominy and bring to a boil. Reduce the heat to low, cover, and simmer for 15 minutes. Taste and add more water or salt if necessary.

6 Serve hot in individual bowls. Add lime juice to taste, and garnish as desired.

Boneless, skinless chicken breasts, 2

Reduced-sodium chicken broth, 4 to 5 cups

Onion, 1 small, chopped

Garlic, 2 cloves, chopped

Canola oil, 1 tablespoon

Hominy, 1 (29-ounce) can, drained

Tomatoes, 2 large

Chipotle chili in adobo sauce, 1, finely chopped

Chili powder, 1 tablespoon

Toppings:
Cilantro leaves, chopped

Cabbage, finely sliced

Radishes, thinly sliced

Onion, chopped

Limes, 2, cut into wedges

Per Serving
Calories, 134
Total fat, 3.5 g
   Saturated fat, 0.5 g
   Trans fat, 0.0 g
   Polyunsaturated fat, 1.1 g
   Monounsaturated fat, 1.6 g
Total carbohydrate, 15 g
   Dietary fiber, 3 g
   Sugars, 4 g
Protein, 10 g
Sodium, 389 mg

leek, potato, and sausage soup

Potatoes, 6, peeled and julienned

Spicy turkey Italian sausage, ½ pound, casings removed, optional

Garlic, minced, 2 teaspoons, divided

Ground cumin, 2 teaspoons, divided

Dried basil, 2 teaspoons, divided

Leeks, 3

Butter, 3 tablespoons

Canola oil, 1½ teaspoons

Nonfat half-and-half, 1 cup, optional

Milk (1 percent), 5 cups

This is my husband, Tom's, favorite soup to make, and our family loves it! Because sausage can be very salty, salt is not typically needed. Before serving the soup, taste and add salt only if necessary. You can make the soup vegetarian just by omitting the sausage. —Maya

---

Prep Time: 30 minutes | **Total Time:** 2 hours | **8 Servings**

1 Place the potatoes in a pan with water just to cover. Bring to a boil and cook for 30 minutes, or until potatoes are easily pierced with a knife. Remove from heat, but do not drain the water.

2 In a frying pan over medium heat, cook the sausage, along with 1 teaspoon of the garlic, 1 teaspoon of the cumin, and 1 teaspoon of the basil. Break the sausage into small chunks and cook until well done. Remove the sausage to a plate lined with paper towels and blot thoroughly to remove excess grease.

3 Cut the leeks lengthwise and wash them thoroughly to remove any trapped grit. Chop the white and light green parts into very small pieces and rinse in a strainer.

4 Put the butter in a heavy Dutch oven with the canola oil to keep it from burning. Add the remaining garlic, cumin, and basil and cook for 2 minutes over medium heat. Add the leeks and sauté until translucent.

5 Add the sausage, the half-and-half, and the potatoes, along with their cooking water. Mix well and cook for 5 to 10 minutes. Add the milk and bring to a boil. Reduce heat and simmer for 30 minutes. Serve in soup bowls.

Per Serving (with sausage)
Calories, 252
Total fat, 9.5 g
    Saturated fat, 4.5 g
    Trans fat, 0.3 g
    Polyunsaturated fat, 1.2 g
    Monounsaturated fat, 3.0 g
Total carbohydrate, 31 g
    Dietary fiber, 2 g
    Sugars, 10 g
Protein, 12 g
Sodium, 349 mg

Per Serving (without sausage)
Calories, 210
Total fat, 6.9 g
    Saturated fat, 3.8 g
    Trans fat, 0.2 g
    Polyunsaturated fat, 0.6 g
    Monounsaturated fat, 2.1 g
Total carbohydrate, 31 g
    Dietary fiber, 2 g
    Sugars, 10 g
Protein, 7 g
Sodium, 117 mg

aguadito

In Peru, this soup is called "aguadito," which means watery. It is similar to a traditional chicken and rice soup. I call this the miracle soup; if you have unexpected guests, all you have to do is add more water and it stretches to serve them all. The flavor does not even change much in the process! The original recipe calls for chicken, meat, or seafood. This quick version includes imitation crabmeat instead. It is easy, economical, and just as nutritious. —Maya

Prep Time: 30 minutes | **Total Time:** 1 hour | **10 Servings**

1 Coat a large, heavy pot with nonstick cooking spray. Sauté the onion, garlic, cumin, and pepper over medium heat until the onion is translucent.

2 Purée the cilantro leaves in a blender with ½ cup water.

3 Add the cilantro purée and brown rice to the onion mixture. Continue to sauté for a few minutes to allow the rice to absorb the flavor of the cilantro. Then add the remaining ingredients, except the salt and the imitation crabmeat. Bring to a boil. Reduce heat and cook, covered, for 25 to 30 minutes, or until the rice is cooked.

4 Add the imitation crabmeat and continue cooking for an additional 5 to 10 minutes.

5 Taste and add salt if needed. Serve with lime wedges for squeezing over the soup or with the "Almost True" Peruvian Yellow Hot Pepper Sauce (page 15).

Red onion, chopped, 1 cup

Garlic, minced, 1 tablespoon

Ground cumin, 1 teaspoon

Ground black pepper, ¼ teaspoon

Cilantro leaves, 1 cup, packed

Water, ½ cup

Brown rice, uncooked, ½ cup

Celery, finely chopped, 1 cup

Green bell pepper, stemmed, seeded, and chopped, 1 cup

Red bell pepper, stemmed, seeded, and chopped, 1 cup

Frozen corn, 1 cup

Frozen peas and carrots, 1 cup

Reduced-sodium chicken broth, 10 cups

Light beer, 1 bottle, optional

Imitation crabmeat, 2 cups

Salt, to taste

Limes, 2, cut into wedges

"Almost True" Peruvian Yellow Hot Pepper Sauce (page 15), optional

Per Serving
Calories, 111
Total fat, 0.7 g
  Saturated fat, 0.1 g
  Trans fat, 0.0 g
  Polyunsaturated fat, 0.2 g
  Monounsaturated fat, 0.2 g
Total carbohydrate, 20 g
  Dietary fiber, 2 g
  Sugars, 5 g
Protein, 6 g
Sodium, 745 mg

peruvian butternut squash soup

Butternut squash, 2 pounds, peeled, seeded, and coarsely chopped, or 2 (14-ounce) boxes frozen butternut squash

Yams or sweet potatoes, 4 large, peeled and coarsely chopped

Butter, 2 tablespoons

All-purpose flour, 3 tablespoons

Milk (skim), 2 cups, at room temperature

Garlic, 1 clove, minced

Ground white pepper, ⅛ teaspoon

Ground nutmeg, ⅛ teaspoon

Salt, ½ teaspoon, or to taste

Reduced-sodium chicken or vegetable broth, 1 cup

Fat-free evaporated milk, 1 (12-ounce) can

Dried mint leaves, crumbled, 1 teaspoon

Feta or goat cheese, crumbled, 4 tablespoons

Baked croutons, optional

My mom used to prepare this soup for us on cold winter days, and we absolutely loved it. —Maya

Prep Time: 15 minutes | **Total Time:** 1 hour | **8 Servings**

1 Put butternut squash and yams in a pot with just enough water to cover. Bring to a boil and cook until very soft. Put them and their cooking water in a blender and blend thoroughly. Alternately, you can use a hand blender inside the pot.

2 In a large heavy pot over medium-high heat, melt the butter and sauté the flour, stirring constantly with a wooden spoon for 4 to 5 minutes, or until the flour is totally cooked. Gradually add the milk, stirring constantly to prevent lumps from forming. Add the garlic, white pepper, ground nutmeg, and salt, and cook for about 2 more minutes.

3 Pour the blended butternut squash and yam mixture and chicken broth into the pot. Bring to a boil. Reduce heat and simmer for 10 minutes.

4 Add the evaporated milk and crumbled mint leaves and stir well to incorporate. Taste and add additional salt if needed, remembering that the feta cheese will be added on top. Cook for 5 more minutes or until heated through.

5 Serve in soup bowls. Top each serving with crumbled cheese and croutons.

Per Serving
Calories, 242
Total fat, 4.4 g
    Saturated fat, 2.7 g
    Trans fat, 0.2 g
    Polyunsaturated fat, 0.3 g
    Monounsaturated fat, 1.0 g
Total carbohydrate, 43 g
    Dietary fiber, 6 g
    Sugars, 12 g
Protein, 9 g
Sodium, 376 mg

mexican-style beef soup

Lean beef stew meat, 1 pound, cut into bite-sized pieces

Onion, 1, quartered

Potatoes, 2, peeled and cut in half

Yams or sweet potatoes, 2, peeled and cut into thick slices

Carrots, 4, peeled and sliced

Corn, 1 ear, cut into 6 pieces

Celery, 4 stalks, sliced

Zucchini, 2, unpeeled, cut into medium-sized pieces

Cabbage, ¼, cut into 4 pieces

Water, 5 to 6 cups

Salt, ½ teaspoon, or to taste

Cooking this delicious soup in a slow cooker makes it a snap to prepare. However, it can also be cooked on the stovetop to shorten cooking time. If you prefer stronger flavors, it can be served with flavorful spices and herbs, such as chopped cilantro, finely chopped onion, hot pepper, or salsas, such as those described in the section on sauces on pages 12-17.
—Martín

Prep Time: 20 minutes | **Total Time:** 5 to 6 hours | **6 Servings**

1 Put all the ingredients in a large slow cooker, placing the meat on the bottom and continuing through the cabbage. Add 5 to 6 cups water and ½ teaspoon salt.

2 Set the slow cooker on high for 4 hours or medium for 6 hours.

3 At the end of the cooking time, taste and adjust seasonings as needed. Stir very gently to prevent vegetables from falling apart. Serve in soup bowls and add condiments on top to add more flavor, if desired.

Per Serving
Calories, 247
Total fat, 3.7 g
   Saturated fat, 1.4 g
   Trans fat, 0.2 g
   Polyunsaturated fat, 0.5 g
   Monounsaturated fat, 1.7 g
Total carbohydrate, 36 g
   Dietary fiber, 7 g
   Sugars, 7 g
Protein, 19 g
Sodium, 306 mg

side
dishes

rice with green pigeon peas and coconut milk

Extra long grain brown rice, uncooked, 2 cups

Canola oil, 1 tablespoon

Frozen green pigeon peas, 1 cup, or 1 (10.5-ounce) can, drained, liquid reserved

Malena's Sofrito (page 10), 1 tablespoon

Light coconut milk, 1 cup

Water, 2 cups

Green pigeon peas are called "guandules" in Panama and "gandules" in Puerto Rico. Look in Hispanic markets for canned or frozen pigeon peas. They look like small green peas with eyes. For this recipe, reserve the liquid in the can to add at the end. If you have my sofrito on hand (page 10), use 1 tablespoon. If not, just chop one garlic clove and a tablespoon of cilantro leaves. My 8-year-old son, Alexander, told me that he was sure this dish would be perfect for kids since it's his favorite. —Malena

Prep Time: 5 minutes | **Total Time:** 1 hour | **7 Servings**

1 Rinse the rice thoroughly and set aside.

2 In a heavy 4-quart pot with a lid, heat the oil over high heat and sauté the pigeon peas for 1 to 3 minutes, lightly browning them.

3 Add the rice, sofrito, coconut milk, the reserved liquid from the peas, and 2 cups of water and stir to combine. Bring to a boil and cook for 15 minutes over medium heat, uncovered.

4 Reduce heat to the lowest setting, cover, and cook for 30 minutes.

5 Uncover and stir with a fork to thoroughly combine the rice and the peas.

6 Cover the pot and cook for an additional 15 to 20 minutes.

Per Serving
Calories, 258
Total fat, 5.7 g
    Saturated fat, 1.6 g
    Trans fat, 0.0 g
    Polyunsaturated fat, 1.4 g
    Monounsaturated fat, 2.2 g
Total carbohydrate, 46 g
    Dietary fiber, 4 g
    Sugars, 2 g
Protein, 6 g
Sodium, 23 mg

m&m's refried beans

This is a healthy and delicious alternative to the traditional Mexican recipe. You can cook the beans in a regular pot, pressure cooker, or slow cooker. —Maya and Malena

Prep Time: 20 minutes (plus time to soak beans) | **Total Time:** 3 to 4 hours | **10 Servings**

Dried pinto beans, 1 pound (about 2 cups)

Garlic, 2 cloves, divided

Water, 6 cups

Yellow or red onion, ½, finely chopped

Vegetable oil, 1 tablespoon

Salt, to taste

Ground cumin, ½ teaspoon

1 Rinse the beans and let them soak overnight. If possible, change the water several times.

2 Drain the beans and put them into a large, heavy pot or pressure cooker with one clove garlic. Add 6 cups of water to cover beans. Bring to a boil. If cooking in a conventional pot, reduce heat to a simmer, and cook, partially covered, for 2 to 2½ hours. If using a pressure cooker, you will need to cook for about an hour, depending on the instructions for your device. If using a slow cooker, cook on high for 3 to 4 hours.

3 Drain the cooked beans, reserving the cooking water. Using a blender or food processor, purée the beans in batches, adding about ½ to 1 cup of the cooking water at a time until they are smooth.

4 Heat the oil in a large pot and sauté the onion until golden brown.

5 Finely chop the remaining clove garlic. Add the garlic, salt, and cumin to the pot and combine.

6 When the onion is golden brown, add the puréed beans. Cook for 10 to 15 minutes, or until the beans thicken. Taste and adjust the seasoning as necessary.

Per Serving
Calories, 169
Total fat, 2.1 g
   Saturated fat, 0.3 g
   Trans fat, 0.0 g
   Polyunsaturated fat, 0.6 g
   Monounsaturated fat, 1.0 g
Total carbohydrate, 29 g
   Dietary fiber, 10 g
   Sugars, 1 g
Protein, 10 g
Sodium, 2 mg

cuban-style black beans and rice

My good friend Carmita Timiraos, whom I call my Cuban mother, taught me how to make this tasty dish.

Making your own black beans is easy and economical. First, presoak the beans overnight, covering with water. Before cooking, strain the beans and add fresh water. You can cook the beans on the stovetop, in a pressure cooker, or in a slow cooker. To cook on the stovetop, add 3 cups of water for each cup of beans and cook over medium heat, partially covered, for 1½ to 2 hours, skimming off any foam. In a pressure cooker, the beans should be done in about half an hour. In a slow cooker, use 3 cups of water for each cup of beans and cook on low for 8 hours.
—Maya

Canola oil, 1 tablespoon

Red onion, finely chopped, ½ cup

Garlic, minced, 1 tablespoon

Ground cumin, ¼ teaspoon

Dried oregano, ¼ teaspoon

Sea salt, ¼ teaspoon

Black beans, cooked, 3 cups, or 2 (15-ounce) cans black beans, drained, liquid reserved

Bay leaves, 2

Brown or white rice, cooked, 3 cups

Extra-virgin olive oil, 6 teaspoons

Prep Time: 10 minutes | **Total Time:** 30 minutes (plus time to cook beans) | **6 Servings**

1 Heat the canola oil in a large, heavy pot and cook the onion until translucent. Add the garlic, cumin, oregano, and salt. Sauté for 2 minutes.

2 Add the beans and bay leaves. If using canned beans, add a small amount of the liquid along with the beans. Cook for 5 to 8 minutes on medium heat.

3 Remove the bay leaves.

4 To serve, put about ½ cup of cooked rice on a plate and top with ½ cup of black beans. Drizzle 1 teaspoon of olive oil on top.

Per Serving
Calories, 291
Total fat, 8.2 g
    Saturated fat, 1.1 g
    Trans fat, 0.0 g
    Polyunsaturated fat, 1.7 g
    Monounsaturated fat, 5.1 g
Total carbohydrate, 45 g
    Dietary fiber, 9 g
    Sugars, 3 g
Protein, 10 g
Sodium, 105 mg

brown rice with almonds

Long grain brown rice, uncooked, 1 cup

Canola oil, 1 tablespoon

Onion, chopped, ¼ cup

Garlic, 1 clove, finely chopped

Fat-free low-sodium vegetable broth, 2 cups

Cilantro leaves, chopped, 2 tablespoons, optional

Ground cumin, ¼ teaspoon

Salt, ½ teaspoon, or to taste

Ground black pepper, ¼ teaspoon

Slivered almonds, ⅓ cup

Almonds are a rich source of protein and fiber and add taste and texture to dishes. You can also add raisins, sliced red onion, chopped basil, or dried cranberries to this recipe. Try this dish cold as a salad, mixed with baby spinach or arugula and tossed with olive oil and freshly squeezed lemon juice. —Martín

Prep Time: 10 minutes | **Total Time:** 1 hour | **4 Servings**

1 Rinse the brown rice and set aside.

2 Heat the canola oil in a 2-quart pot over high heat. Sauté the onion until translucent. Add the garlic. Continue cooking until the onion and garlic start to brown.

3 Add the rice and mix well. Add broth, cilantro, cumin, salt, and pepper and bring to a boil. Cook for 5 minutes, then reduce heat to low, cover, and cook for 40 minutes, or until the liquid is fully absorbed.

4 Add the almonds and stir lightly with a fork. Cover and continue to cook on low heat for an additional 10 minutes before serving.

Per Serving
Calories, 273
Total fat, 9.8 g
    Saturated fat, 0.9 g
    Trans fat, 0.0 g
    Polyunsaturated fat, 2.7 g
    Monounsaturated fat, 5.8 g
Total carbohydrate, 40 g
    Dietary fiber, 4 g
    Sugars, 2 g
Protein, 6 g
Sodium, 369 mg

beets with lime sauce

This exquisite sauce is also good with asparagus, string beans, carrots, and other cooked vegetables. Instead of reduced-fat sour cream, you can use Mexican crema, a very mild cream that is less sour than sour cream. It is found in Hispanic markets and in some general supermarkets.

You can also roast the beets—an easy technique that gives great flavor and makes peeling them easy. Preheat the oven to 375 degrees. Wash and stem beets and place on a large piece of foil. Drizzle with olive oil or canola oil and fold the foil over and seal to make a packet. Roast for one hour, or until tender. When they're cool enough to handle, you can easily peel off the skins. —Martín

Prep Time: 15 minutes | **Total Time:** 30 minutes | **6 Servings**

Beets, 4 to 6

Olive oil, 1 tablespoon

White or yellow onion, finely chopped, 1 cup

Garlic, 2 cloves, minced

Reduced-fat sour cream or Mexican crema, 1 cup

Dijon mustard, 3 tablespoons

Salt, ¼ teaspoon, or to taste

Ground black pepper, ¼ teaspoon, or to taste

Freshly squeezed lime juice, ¼ cup

Flat leaf parsley, chopped, ¼ cup

1. To cook the beets, rinse and scrub them. Put them in a pot with water to cover and bring to a boil. Lower heat to medium, cover, and cook until tender and easily pierced with a knife or fork, approximately 20 minutes. Drain, peel, and slice them. Set aside.

2. Heat the olive oil in a skillet over medium heat and cook the onion until translucent. Add garlic and sauté for 1 to 2 minutes.

3. Add the sour cream, mustard, salt, and pepper. Stir for a couple of minutes until well combined.

4. Add the lime juice just before serving. Add salt, if needed.

5. Arrange the beets on a serving plate and carefully pour the sauce on top without covering them entirely. Garnish with chopped parsley. Serve at room temperature.

Per Serving
Calories, 125
Total fat, 6.0 g
    Saturated fat, 3.0 g
    Trans fat, 0.0 g
    Polyunsaturated fat, 0.5 g
    Monounsaturated fat, 2.4 g
Total carbohydrate, 14 g
    Dietary fiber, 2 g
    Sugars, 9 g
Protein, 5 g
Sodium, 360 mg

quinoa salad

Quinoa, uncooked, 1 cup

Water, 2 cups

Extra-virgin olive oil, 3 tablespoons

Red wine vinegar, 3 tablespoons

Roma tomatoes, 3, finely diced

Green onions, 4 to 5, finely chopped, or ½ red onion, finely chopped

Ground white pepper, to taste

Queso fresco or feta cheese, crumbled, ¼ cup

Juice of 1 lemon

Cilantro leaves, chopped, ¼ cup

Salt, to taste

Quinoa is native to Peru, and the Incas considered it a sacred food. It does not contain wheat, so it is ideal for those on a gluten-free diet. One cup of uncooked quinoa will yield about 4 cups when cooked. This recipe calls for queso fresco, which is a soft, moist cheese with a mild flavor.
—Maya

Prep Time: 30 minutes | **Total Time:** 1 hour and 30 minutes | **6 Servings**

1 Wash the quinoa in a large bowl of fresh cold water, rubbing the grains with your fingers. Drain the quinoa using a fine mesh colander and rinse again using fresh water. Wash the quinoa four to five times, until the water is clear and no foam appears.

2 Bring 2 cups of water to a boil, and add the quinoa. Cook for 1 minute, stir, reduce heat to low, and cover. Cook for about 15 minutes, or until the grains burst and look like half moons and the water has been absorbed.

3 Pour the cooked quinoa into a glass container and refrigerate for at least 30 minutes.

4 In the meantime, put the olive oil and the vinegar into a glass container and whisk until well combined. Add the diced tomatoes, green onions, and white pepper, to taste. Refrigerate for 15 minutes.

5 When the quinoa is chilled, add the olive oil mixture, queso fresco, lemon juice, and cilantro. Stir to combine. Let sit for about 15 more minutes to allow the flavors to meld. Taste and add salt if desired.

Per Serving
Calories, 202
Total fat, 9.9 g
  Saturated fat, 1.9 g
  Trans fat, 0.0 g
  Polyunsaturated fat, 1.9 g
  Monounsaturated fat, 6.0 g
Total carbohydrate, 23 g
  Dietary fiber, 4 g
  Sugars, 4 g
Protein, 6 g
Sodium, 50 mg

American Cancer Society

Quinoa contains a chemical compound called saponin,
which has a bitter taste. That is why it is important to
wash the quinoa thoroughly before cooking to remove
the saponin, unless the package says the quinoa has been
prewashed. For the best flavor, I like to use the original
quinoa and not the "quick cooking" version.

plantain bread

Plantains, 3 ripe

Brown sugar, ½ teaspoon

Butter, 1 tablespoon, softened

Ground cinnamon, 2 teaspoons, divided

**Reduced-fat Monterey jack or
mozzarella cheese,** 1 cup

Plantains are very popular in Central America and can be used in many ways. This recipe comes from my dear Aunt Mathy and is absolutely delicious. You can find plantains that are slightly green at the store and let them ripen at home. The plantains are ripe when the peel turns black. —Malena

Prep Time: 10 minutes | **Total Time:** 45 minutes | **6 Servings**

1 Preheat the oven to 325 degrees.

2 Cut plantains into three segments, leaving the peel intact. It's not necessary to cut the tips off. Place the plantains in a pan with enough water to cover. Bring to a boil and cook for 10 minutes, or until they are soft and the peel is practically falling off on its own.

3 Remove the peel with a knife and place the plantains in a bowl. Add the brown sugar, butter, and 1 teaspoon of the ground cinnamon. Mash well to make a purée.

4 Grease an 8-by-8-inch square baking pan. Put half of the purée (about 1½ cups) into the pan and spread out. Sprinkle the cheese on top. Put the rest of the plantain purée on top of the cheese and spread carefully. Top with the remaining teaspoon of ground cinnamon. Bake for 20 minutes.

5 Remove the pan from the oven and cut into squares. Serve hot as an accompaniment to stews or as a snack.

Per Serving
Calories, 213
Total fat, 6.1 g
    Saturated fat, 3.6 g
    Trans fat, 0.1 g
    Polyunsaturated fat, 0.2 g
    Monounsaturated fat, 1.5 g
Total carbohydrate, 39 g
    Dietary fiber, 3 g
    Sugars, 17 g
Protein, 6 g
Sodium, 183 mg

grilled veggies

I like to use an assortment of different colored bell peppers: red, yellow, green, even orange if I can find them. You can add spice by including jalapeño or serrano chilies or add other favorite vegetables. You can cook these vegetables on a griddle or on an actual charcoal or gas grill, using a grill basket. —Maya

Bell peppers of any color, 2 to 3

Yellow squash, 1 to 2

Zucchini, 1 to 2

Onion, 1, cut into six pieces

Lemon pepper seasoning, to taste

Prep Time: 15 minutes | **Total Time:** 30 minutes | **6 Servings**

1 Cut off the stem of each bell pepper and remove the seeds. Slice the peppers into thin rings.

2 Slice the yellow squash and zucchini into thin discs.

3 Spray the peppers and vegetables with olive oil-flavored nonstick cooking spray. Place on a griddle or grill over medium-high heat. Sprinkle with lemon pepper seasoning. Cook until the vegetables are browned, about 5 minutes on each side.

Per Serving
Calories, 32
Total fat, 0.3 g
    Saturated fat, 0.1 g
    Trans fat, 0.0 g
    Polyunsaturated fat, 0.1 g
    Monounsaturated fat, 0.0 g
Total carbohydrate, 7 g
    Dietary fiber, 2 g
    Sugars, 4 g
Protein, 2 g
Sodium, 6 mg

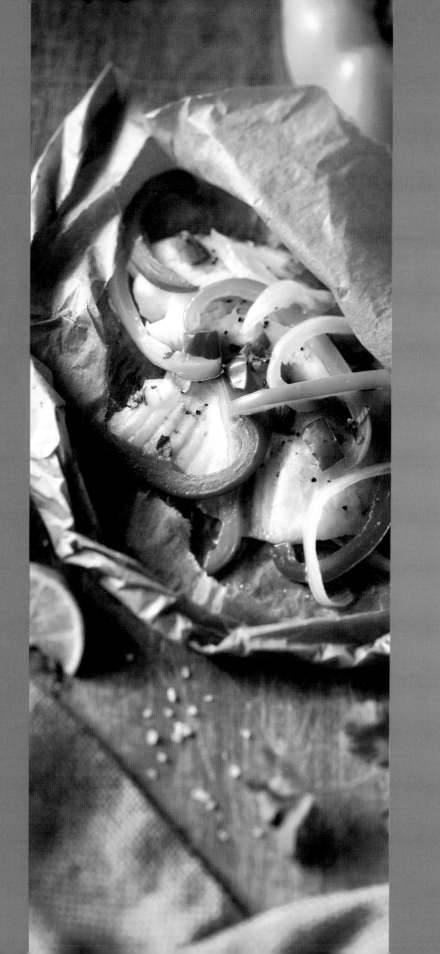

main
dishes

flounder stuffed with crabmeat

White Sauce (page 17), ½ cup

Flounder or other white fish (such as tilapia or red snapper), 4 fillets

Fish seasoning, 1 tablespoon

Crabmeat, 1 (6-ounce) can, drained

Frozen green peas, 1 cup

Asparagus, chopped, 1 cup

Roasted marinated red peppers, chopped, 2 tablespoons

Fresh basil, chopped, 1 teaspoon

Capers, drained, 2 teaspoons

Bread crumbs, ¼ cup

This recipe is ideal for dinner guests. You should be able to find fish seasoning in the spice section or the seafood section at the supermarket. Roasted red peppers also are available in most supermarkets. Look for roasted red peppers that are marinated (usually sold in jars), which will have more flavor. —Malena

Prep Time: 20 minutes | **Total Time:** 45 minutes | **4 Servings**

1 Preheat oven to 350 degrees.

2 Prepare the white sauce and set aside.

3 Spray the bottom of a baking dish with nonstick cooking spray. Place the fillets in the baking dish and season them with the fish seasoning. Place pieces of crabmeat over each fillet, spreading them evenly.

4 Roll up each fillet and secure it with long toothpicks. If using a fish that is difficult to roll without breaking, simply leave flat.

5 In a bowl, combine the peas, asparagus, red peppers, basil, and capers. Sprinkle this mixture over the fish. Cover the fillets with white sauce and sprinkle bread crumbs over the top.

6 Bake, uncovered, for 25 minutes.

Per Serving
Calories, 280
Total fat, 9.3 g
  Saturated fat, 5.0 g
  Trans fat, 0.2 g
  Polyunsaturated fat, 1.2 g
  Monounsaturated fat, 2.6 g
Total carbohydrate, 18 g
  Dietary fiber, 3 g
  Sugars, 6 g
Protein, 31 g
Sodium, 1216 mg

oven-baked pachamanca

This recipe originated in the Inca culture of Peru. "Pachamanca" is a word in Quechua, the language of the Incas. "Pacha" means earth, and "manca" means pot. The traditional way of preparing pachamanca is in a hole in the ground. The hole is lined with hot stones, and corn husk–wrapped meats and vegetables are put in the hole and covered with more hot stones. The version offered here is an easy and fast alternative for preparing this meal. When my boys were little, they loved this dish because the foil packets were like surprise packages. Now, my son, Chris, who is a vegetarian, really likes it when I prepare this recipe with just veggies. —Maya

Prep Time: 20 minutes | **Total Time:** 1 hour | **6 Servings**

Cilantro leaves, 2 cups

Fresh spinach, 1 cup

Garlic, 3 cloves, minced

Ground cumin, 1 tablespoon

Salt, ½ teaspoon

Ground black pepper, ¼ teaspoon

Water, ½ cup

Chicken thighs and drumsticks, 3 each, skin removed

Carrots, sliced, 1 cup

Frozen green peas, 1 cup

Frozen corn, 1 cup

Potatoes, unpeeled, diced, 1 cup

1. Place cilantro, spinach, garlic, cumin, salt, pepper, and ½ cup water in a blender. Blend to sauce consistency. Pour one-third of the mixture into a bowl and the other two-thirds into another bowl.

2. Place the chicken in the smaller bowl of sauce, mixing well to cover. Set aside. Place the vegetables in the second bowl of sauce and mix well.

3. Cut six pieces of aluminum foil into 12-by-12-inch squares.

4. Place a piece of chicken in the center of each piece of foil and top with a scoop of vegetables. Fold the edges of the foil in to form a packet. Make sure to fold the edges well so that there are no gaps or leaks.

5. Place all the packets on a baking sheet and bake for 45 to 50 minutes at 375 degrees. There is no need to preheat the oven.

Per Serving
Calories, 175
Total fat, 4.6 g
    Saturated fat, 1.2 g
    Trans fat, 0.0 g
    Polyunsaturated fat, 1.1 g
    Monounsaturated fat, 1.7 g
Total carbohydrate, 18 g
    Dietary fiber, 4 g
    Sugars, 3 g
Protein, 16 g
Sodium, 281 mg

fish à papillot

This is one of my favorite recipes. Wrapping the fish with parchment paper optimizes the flavor of the fish and the vegetables. Plus, it's fun to put together. These can be baked in the oven or cooked on a grill. If cooking on a grill, wrap the fish in aluminum foil instead. —Martin

Prep Time: 20 minutes | **Total Time:** 30 to 45 minutes | **6 Servings**

1. Preheat the oven to 350 degrees.

2. Season the fish fillets with salt, pepper, and cumin. Set aside.

3. Tear off six 15-inch square pieces of parchment paper. Fold in half to make a crease.

4. Place 1 teaspoon olive oil to one side of the crease on each piece of parchment paper. Top with a few pieces of onion and one fish fillet. Top the fillet with about 1 tablespoon of chopped tomato and cover with bell peppers, more onion, and a sprinkle of cilantro. Squeeze lime juice over the top. To close, fold over parchment and crimp edges well to seal, forming the shape of a half-moon.

5. Spread the packets on two cookie sheets. Do not stack the packets on top of each other. Bake for approximately 15 to 20 minutes, or until the packets have puffed up with steam. If cooking on a grill, wrap the fish in foil and cook on a hot grill for 10 to 15 minutes.

6. Before opening the packets, carefully punch a few holes in them with a fork or sharp knife to allow some of the steam to escape. Serve in the packets or remove to a plate or dish.

Firm white fish (such as tilapia, flounder, or trout), 6 fillets

Salt and ground black pepper

Ground cumin, ¼ teaspoon

Olive oil, 6 teaspoons

White onion, 1 large, cut into strips

Tomato, 1 large, chopped

Yellow bell pepper, 1, stemmed, seeded, and cut into strips

Green bell pepper, 1, stemmed, seeded, and cut into strips

Red bell pepper, 1, stemmed, seeded, and cut into strips

Cilantro leaves, chopped, ½ cup

Limes, 2 to 3

Per Serving
Calories, 183
Total fat, 6.1 g
   Saturated fat, 1.0 g
   Trans fat, 0.0 g
   Polyunsaturated fat, 1.2 g
   Monounsaturated fat, 3.6 g
Total carbohydrate, 9 g
   Dietary fiber, 2 g
   Sugars, 5 g
Protein, 23 g
Sodium, 99 mg

chilies with shrimp and spinach stuffing

Poblano chilies, 6

Medium fresh or frozen shrimp, ½ pound, peeled, deveined, tails removed

Garlic, 2 cloves, divided

Onion, finely chopped, ¾ cup, divided

Salt, ½ teaspoon, or to taste

Ground black pepper, ¼ teaspoon, or to taste

Dried oregano, ¼ teaspoon

Baby spinach leaves, 3 cups

Reduced-fat sour cream, ¼ cup

Oaxaca or Monterey jack cheese, shredded, ½ cup

Black beans, cooked, 2 cups, or 1 (15-ounce) can black beans, rinsed and drained

Light cream cheese, 4 ounces, softened

If you cook your black beans from scratch, save some of the cooking water—it can be used to thin the sauce at the end of this recipe.

Per Serving
Calories, 237
Total fat, 8.6 g
    Saturated fat, 5.0 g
    Trans fat, 0.0 g
    Polyunsaturated fat, 0.7 g
    Monounsaturated fat, 2.1 g
Total carbohydrate, 25 g
    Dietary fiber, 7 g
    Sugars, 7 g
Protein, 17 g
Sodium, 408 mg

Oaxaca cheese is a mild, white cheese from Mexico. If you can't find it, Monterey jack is a good substitute. —Martín

Prep Time: 30 minutes | **Total Time:** 1 hour | **6 Servings**

1 Roast the chilies according to the instructions on page 6. Leave the stems on when you devein them. Set aside.

2 Preheat oven to 250 degrees.

3 Coarsely chop the shrimp. If using frozen shrimp, thaw and dry first.

4 Chop one clove of garlic. Spray a frying pan with nonstick cooking spray and sauté ½ cup of the onion over medium heat until translucent. Add the chopped garlic and cook for 3 to 5 minutes.

5 Add the chopped shrimp to the pan and cook for 2 minutes. Season with salt, pepper, and oregano. Add the spinach and cook for 3 minutes, or until wilted. Add the sour cream and Oaxaca cheese, mix well, and cook for 2 more minutes. Remove from heat.

6 Stuff the chilies with the shrimp mixture and place in a baking dish. Cover with aluminum foil and place them in the oven while you prepare the sauce, approximately 20 minutes.

7 Mince the remaining clove of garlic. Spray a pan with nonstick cooking spray and sauté the remaining ¼ cup onion over medium heat. When the onion is translucent, add the garlic and the beans. Stir to combine and let cook for 5 minutes. Taste and add salt if necessary.

8 Place the bean mixture in a blender with the cream cheese and blend. If sauce is too thick, add 2 to 3 tablespoons water or the beans' cooking liquid. Serve the chilies smothered with the bean sauce.

garlic shrimp

This is a quick and delicious recipe for special occasions. I like to serve it with rice and grilled vegetables. —Martín

Prep Time: 15 minutes | **Total Time:** 20 minutes | **4 Servings**

1 Rinse the shrimp. Pat dry with a paper towel, and set aside. If the shrimp is frozen, thaw first.

2 In a blender, process the mayonnaise, garlic, and mustard for 1 minute or until well combined.

3 Heat the oil in a frying pan over medium heat and sauté the shrimp for 2 minutes. Add the garlic mixture and stir well. Cook the shrimp for about 3 minutes or until they turn pink. Taste and add salt if necessary.

4 Garnish with fresh parsley and serve hot.

Medium shrimp, 1 pound, peeled, deveined, tails removed

Reduced-fat mayonnaise, ⅓ cup

Garlic, 1 bulb, cloves peeled (about 10 cloves)

Dijon mustard, 2 tablespoons

Olive oil, 1 tablespoon

Salt, to taste

Flat leaf parsley, chopped, 1 tablespoon

Per Serving
Calories, 186
Total fat, 10.9 g
    Saturated fat, 1.7 g
    Trans fat, 0.0 g
    Polyunsaturated fat, 4.2 g
    Monounsaturated fat, 4.4 g
Total carbohydrate, 5 g
    Dietary fiber, 0 g
    Sugars, 1 g
Protein, 17 g
Sodium, 458 mg

chalaca-style fish

Tilapia or other white fish, 4 fillets

Salt and ground black pepper

Ground cumin, ¼ teaspoon, plus additional for seasoning fish

Onion, 1, sliced

Garlic, 1 clove, crushed

Tomatoes, 3, quartered, or 1 (15-ounce) can Italian-style stewed tomatoes

Light or dark brown sugar, 1 tablespoon

Bay leaves, 2

Red or Marsala wine, ¼ cup

Flat leaf parsley, finely chopped, ¼ cup

This is one of my favorite Peruvian dishes. "Chalaca" refers to the area of Callao, the main seaport in Peru. I like to serve the fish smothered with the onions and tomato sauce, accompanied with a simple green salad or rice and peas. —Maya

Prep Time: 15 minutes | **Total Time:** 30 minutes | **4 Servings**

1. Season the fish fillets with salt, pepper, and a sprinkle of cumin. Coat a skillet with nonstick cooking spray. Over medium-high heat, cook the fish until browned on both sides. Remove the fillets from the skillet and set aside.

2. In the same skillet, sauté the onion, using more nonstick cooking spray if necessary. When translucent, add the garlic, ¼ teaspoon cumin, and salt and pepper. Combine well and set aside.

3. Put the tomatoes in a blender and blend thoroughly. Pour the blended tomatoes in the skillet. Add brown sugar, bay leaves, and wine. Simmer for 5 minutes to allow the tomato to cook. Add the parsley.

4. Carefully place the fish fillets into the skillet, making sure they don't fall apart. Cover and cook for an additional 5 to 7 minutes over low heat.

5. Remove the bay leaves before serving.

Per Serving
Calories, 161
Total fat, 2.5 g
  Saturated fat, 0.8 g
  Trans fat, 0.0 g
  Polyunsaturated fat, 0.6 g
  Monounsaturated fat, 0.9 g
Total carbohydrate, 11 g
  Dietary fiber, 2 g
  Sugars, 8 g
Protein, 24 g
Sodium, 57 mg

fettuccine with poblano sauce

Whole wheat fettuccine, 12 ounces

Poblano chilies, 3

Milk (1 percent), 1½ cups

Light cream cheese, 1 (8-ounce) package

Onion, ½ small, chopped

Garlic, 1 clove

Reduced-sodium chicken bouillon granules, 1 tablespoon, or 1 cube reduced-sodium chicken bouillon

Salt, to taste

Parmesan cheese, grated, ¼ cup

This delicious poblano sauce is a delightful twist on a typical Mexican flavor with a touch of Italian influence. Serve with steamed broccoli or a green salad. —Martín

Prep Time: 30 minutes | **Total Time:** 45 minutes | **6 Servings**

1 Cook the pasta until al dente, following the instructions on the package, and set aside.

2 While the pasta is cooking, roast the chilies according to the instructions on page 6. Remove stems, seeds, and membranes.

3 Combine the roasted poblano chilies with the milk, cream cheese, onion, garlic, and chicken bouillon in a blender. Blend thoroughly.

4 Pour the blended mixture into a large pan and cook over medium heat for about 10 minutes, stirring frequently, until it starts bubbling. When the sauce darkens slightly in color, lower the heat and simmer for about 5 more minutes. Taste and add a pinch of salt if needed. The sauce should not be too thick.

5 Add the sauce to the pasta and mix well. Top with a sprinkle of Parmesan cheese and serve.

Per Serving
Calories, 342
Total fat, 11.3 g
    Saturated fat, 6.0 g
    Trans fat, 0.0 g
    Polyunsaturated fat, 0.8 g
    Monounsaturated fat, 2.9 g
Total carbohydrate, 49 g
    Dietary fiber, 7 g
    Sugars, 8 g
Protein, 16 g
Sodium, 479 mg

garlic-marinated grilled shrimp

Serve these delicious shrimp skewers with grilled vegetables. —Martín

Prep Time: 15 minutes | **Total Time:** 45 minutes to 1 hour (including marination) | **5 Servings**

Large or medium shrimp, 1 pound

Reduced-sodium soy sauce, 2 tablespoons

Olive oil, ⅓ cup

Garlic, finely chopped, 2 tablespoons

Green onions, 2, finely sliced

Salt, ½ teaspoon

Ground black pepper, ½ teaspoon

1 Peel and devein the shrimp, without removing tails, and set aside.

2 In a glass container, combine soy sauce, olive oil, garlic, green onions, salt, and pepper and mix well.

3 Add the shrimp, stir together to coat, and allow to marinate for at least 30 minutes in the refrigerator.

4 Slide the shrimp onto skewers, reserving the marinade mixture.

5 Place skewers on the grill and brush lightly with some of the reserved marinade. Grill for 5 to 7 minutes, turning halfway through, or until the shrimp are pink.

If you are using wooden skewers, be sure to soak them in water for 15 minutes first to prevent them from burning.

Per Serving
Calories, 197
Total fat, 14.9 g
    Saturated fat, 2.1 g
    Trans fat, 0.0 g
    Polyunsaturated fat, 1.7 g
    Monounsaturated fat, 10.5 g
Total carbohydrate, 2 g
    Dietary fiber, 0 g
    Sugars, 1 g
Protein, 14 g
Sodium, 549 mg

shrimp tacos with chipotle

Medium fresh or frozen shrimp, 1 pound, peeled, deveined, tails removed

Red onion, ½ small, finely sliced

Garlic, 2 cloves, finely chopped

Reduced-fat mayonnaise, ½ cup

Chipotle peppers in adobo sauce, 1 to 2, finely chopped

Cilantro leaves, chopped, ¼ cup

Whole wheat tortillas, 8

Avocado, 1, peeled, pitted, and sliced

Tomato, 1, chopped

Carrot, 1, thinly sliced

Cabbage, ¼, shredded

Lime, 1, cut into wedges

Chipotle peppers in adobo sauce can be found in small cans in the Hispanic foods section of the supermarket. They are very spicy. If you have never cooked with them before, start with ½ pepper and taste as you go.

Per Serving
Calories, 239
Total fat, 8.7 g
    Saturated fat, 1.4 g
    Trans fat, 0.0 g
    Polyunsaturated fat, 3.4 g
    Monounsaturated fat, 3.2 g
Total carbohydrate, 29 g
    Dietary fiber, 5 g
    Sugars, 3 g
Protein, 13 g
Sodium, 397 mg

For a more nutritious and satisfying meal, use whole wheat tortillas. Whole wheat tortillas have more fiber and are more filling than white flour tortillas, plus they have fewer calories. —Martín

Prep Time: 10 minutes | **Total Time:** 15 minutes | **8 Servings**

1 Thaw shrimp, if frozen, and rinse with cold water. Pat dry with a paper towel.

2 Coat a skillet with nonstick cooking spray. Over medium-high heat, sauté the onion and garlic for 2 minutes. Add shrimp and sauté for 2 minutes, or until they turn pink.

3 Combine the mayonnaise and chipotle peppers in a bowl. Add this mixture to the shrimp and stir well for 2 minutes.

4 Remove from heat, sprinkle with chopped cilantro, and set aside.

5 Warm the tortillas in the microwave or oven. Spoon approximately six shrimp on top of each tortilla. Serve with two slices of avocado, chopped tomato, a few carrot slices, some shredded cabbage, and a lime wedge for squeezing over top.

sautéed eggplant in italian sauce

Nutritious and delicious, this recipe is an easy and fast way to prepare eggplant. Serve with rice as a main course or alone as a side dish.
—Malena

Eggplant, 1

Olive oil, 1 tablespoon

Onion, 1, chopped

Tomatoes, 2 small, chopped

Garlic, 1 clove, chopped

Reduced-sodium vegetable bouillon granules, 1 tablespoon, or 1 cube reduced-sodium vegetable bouillon

Ground black pepper, ½ teaspoon

Dried Italian seasoning, 1 teaspoon

Flat leaf parsley, chopped, 1 tablespoon

Prep Time: 10 minutes | **Total Time:** 25 minutes | **3 Servings**

1 Cut the tips off the eggplant. Peel and cut into ½-inch cubes.

2 Heat olive oil in a large skillet over medium-high heat and sauté the onion for 1 minute, stirring frequently. Add the eggplant and sauté over medium heat for an additional minute.

3 Add the remaining ingredients except the parsley. Stir, cover, and cook for 10 more minutes. Uncover, add parsley, and stir to combine. Remove from the heat and serve.

Per Serving
Calories, 131
Total fat, 5.1 g
    Saturated fat, 0.7 g
    Trans fat, 0.0 g
    Polyunsaturated fat, 0.7 g
    Monounsaturated fat, 3.3 g
Total carbohydrate, 22 g
    Dietary fiber, 5 g
    Sugars, 9 g
Protein, 2 g
Sodium, 518 mg

peruvian chicken stew

This is one of my favorite traditional Peruvian dishes. I like to serve this stew with rice. I typically make this recipe using a combination of chicken thighs, drumsticks, and breasts. You can use any combination of chicken: a whole cut-up chicken, breasts only, whatever you'd like. —Maya

Prep Time: 30 to 45 minutes | **Total Time:** 1 hour and 30 minutes | **6 Servings**

1 Purée the tomatoes in a blender or food processor. Set aside.

2 Season the chicken with salt, pepper, and ¼ teaspoon of the cumin. Heat 1 tablespoon of the canola oil in a heavy pot and brown the chicken on all sides. Do not cook completely. Remove the chicken once browned and set aside.

3 Add the remaining tablespoon of canola oil to the pot and cook the onion until golden brown. Add the garlic, oregano, and the remaining ¼ teaspoon cumin to the pot.

4 Add the carrots, tomato paste, puréed tomatoes, and bay leaves. Mix well and cook for approximately 10 minutes over medium heat.

5 Add the rest of the ingredients except the peas. Stir to combine. Add the chicken back to the pot. Bring to a boil and let cook for 5 minutes. Reduce heat to low and cover. Allow the stew to cook for 30 minutes, or until the yams and carrots are tender, stirring occasionally. Add more broth or water if the liquid reduces too much.

6 Add the peas and simmer for an additional 5 to 10 minutes. Remove bay leaves before serving.

Tomatoes, 2, or 1 (14-ounce) can whole tomatoes

Chicken thighs, drumsticks, or breasts, 6 pieces, skin removed

Salt and ground black pepper, to taste

Ground cumin, ½ teaspoon, divided

Canola oil, 2 tablespoons, divided

Red onion, ½, finely chopped

Garlic, 1 clove, minced

Dried oregano, ¼ teaspoon

Carrots, 6, sliced

Tomato paste, 3 tablespoons

Bay leaves, 3

Yams or sweet potatoes, 2, peeled and coarsely chopped

Marsala or red wine, ¼ cup, optional

Reduced-sodium chicken broth, 2 cups

Frozen green peas, 1 cup

Adding the peas at the very end keeps them bright green.

Per Serving
Calories, 275
Total fat, 9.0 g
    Saturated fat, 1.5 g
    Trans fat, 0.0 g
    Polyunsaturated fat, 2.4 g
    Monounsaturated fat, 4.4 g
Total carbohydrate, 26 g
    Dietary fiber, 6 g
    Sugars, 7 g
Protein, 23 g
Sodium, 360 mg

mexican ground beef delight

Red onion, 1 medium, finely chopped

Garlic, 2 cloves, finely chopped

Ground beef (95 percent lean), 1 pound

Crushed tomatoes or Roasted Tomato Salsa (page 13), 2 cups

Carrots, 2, diced (approximately 2 cups)

White potatoes, 2, cut into small cubes

Zucchini, 2, diced

Frozen green peas, 1 cup

Bay leaves, 2

Salt and ground black pepper, to taste

This recipe is a good way to use any vegetables you have on hand, and if you have any sofrito in the refrigerator, you can throw that in, too! Use the leanest ground beef possible, or you can use ground turkey breast or vegetarian "meat" crumbles. Serve with rice or use as a filling in tacos. This filling is also good in corn tortillas—roll them up and you're good to go. —Martín

---

Prep Time: 30 minutes | **Total Time:** 45 minutes to 1 hour | **8 Servings**

1 Coat a large frying pan with nonstick cooking spray and sauté the onion and garlic over medium-high heat until golden. Add the meat and cook well, stirring frequently.

2 When meat is browned, add the crushed tomatoes, carrots, and potatoes, mixing well. Reduce heat to medium and cook, uncovered, for 15 minutes.

3 Add the zucchini and peas. If the mixture is too thick, add ¼ cup water.

4 Add the bay leaves and season with salt and pepper. Cook for an additional 15 minutes or until vegetables are soft. Season to taste and remove from heat.

5 Remove the bay leaves and serve.

Per Serving
Calories, 178
Total fat, 3.3 g
    Saturated fat, 1.4 g
    Trans fat, 0.1 g
    Polyunsaturated fat, 0.3 g
    Monounsaturated fat, 1.2 g
Total carbohydrate, 23 g
    Dietary fiber, 4 g
    Sugars, 7 g
Protein, 15 g
Sodium, 84 mg

peruvian covered rice

The meat mixture in this recipe can be prepared the night before. The following day, you'll only need to cook the rice and prepare the white sauce to complete the dish.

For a distinctive presentation, layer the ingredients in cups, rather than a large dish. Unmold, cover with white sauce, and serve immediately.
—Maya

Prep Time: 30 minutes | **Total Time:** 45 minutes | **8 Servings**

1 In a frying pan with no oil, brown the ground beef with salt, pepper, and cumin. Using a colander, drain the grease from the browned meat. Place the meat in a bowl lined with paper towels to absorb the rest of the grease.

2 In the same pan, add the oil and cook the onion until translucent. Add the garlic and cook for 2 to 3 minutes.

3 Add the carrots and cook for 10 to 15 minutes. Add the chopped tomatoes and dried oregano. Add the ground beef, raisins, and peas. Cook on low heat for approximately 20 minutes, or until the carrots are soft.

4 Meanwhile, prepare the white sauce and cook the rice. Set aside.

5 Carefully fold the hard-boiled eggs into the ground beef mixture.

6 Put a thin layer of rice in a flat glass dish. Top with a thick layer of the meat stuffing and then another thin layer of rice. Cover with warm white sauce and sprinkle with fresh chopped parsley. Serve immediately.

Lean ground beef (95 percent lean), 1 pound

Salt, ½ teaspoon

Ground black pepper, ¼ teaspoon

Ground cumin, ½ teaspoon

Canola oil, 2 teaspoons

Red onion, finely chopped, ½ cup

Garlic, minced, ½ teaspoon

Carrots, finely shredded, ½ cup

Tomatoes, 2, chopped, or 1 (14-ounce) can Italian-style stewed tomatoes, chopped

Dried oregano, pinch

Raisins, ½ cup

Frozen green peas, ½ cup

White Sauce (page 17), 2 cups

Hard-boiled eggs, 2, coarsely chopped

Brown or white rice, cooked, 2 cups

Flat leaf parsley, finely chopped, to garnish

Per Serving
Calories, 300
Total fat, 12.9 g
   Saturated fat, 6.4 g
   Trans fat, 0.3 g
   Polyunsaturated fat, 1.2 g
   Monounsaturated fat, 4.7 g
Total carbohydrate, 29 g
   Dietary fiber, 2 g
   Sugars, 11 g
Protein, 18 g
Sodium, 581 mg

chicken and eggplant "lasagna"

Eggplant, 3, peeled and cut lengthwise into ½-inch-thick slices

Salt, 1 teaspoon

Boneless, skinless chicken breasts, 2

Homemade Tomato Sauce (page 16) or store-bought marinara sauce, 4 cups, divided

Olive oil, 1 tablespoon

Water, 2 cups

Reduced-fat mozzarella cheese, shredded, 2 cups, divided

Parmesan cheese, grated, ¼ cup

Bread crumbs, ½ cup

This dish can be made gluten free by just omitting the bread crumbs.

Per Serving
Calories, 215
Total fat, 7.6 g
   Saturated fat, 3.4 g
   Trans fat, 0.0 g
   Polyunsaturated fat, 0.9 g
   Monounsaturated fat, 2.1 g
Total carbohydrate, 23 g
   Dietary fiber, 5 g
   Sugars, 9 g
Protein, 15 g
Sodium, 416 mg

Instead of traditional lasagna noodles, strips of eggplant are used in this dish!
—Malena

Prep Time: 1 hour | **Total Time:** 2 hours | **10 Servings**

1 Preheat the oven to 350 degrees.

2 Place the eggplant strips in a dish with a teaspoon of salt and water to cover, and let them soak for 10 minutes.

3 Place the chicken breasts in a dish and coat with ¼ cup of the tomato sauce.

4 Heat the olive oil in a skillet over medium heat and add the chicken. Cover and cook for 30 minutes, turning the chicken occasionally. Remove the chicken from the skillet and let cool. Once cooled, shred the chicken.

5 In a wide saucepan, bring 2 cups of water to a boil. Working in batches, put three to four strips of the eggplant in the pan and boil for 4 minutes, until cooked but firm, turning halfway through. When done, remove the strips, one at a time, and blot with paper towels to remove excess water.

6 Set aside ¼ cup of the tomato sauce. In the skillet that was used for the chicken, combine the remaining tomato sauce and the shredded chicken. Cover and cook over medium heat for 10 minutes, stirring occasionally.

7 Cover the bottom of a 9-by-13-inch baking pan with the reserved ¼ cup of tomato sauce. Place a layer of eggplant on top of the tomato sauce. Top the eggplant with half of the chicken mixture and ½ cup of the mozzarella cheese. Add another layer of eggplant, the remaining chicken mixture, and ½ cup of the mozzarella cheese. Top with the remaining eggplant.

8 Sprinkle the top with the remaining mozzarella cheese, Parmesan cheese, and bread crumbs. Cover with foil and bake for 35 to 40 minutes. Uncover and bake for an additional 10 minutes. Let cool before serving.

fish with cilantro pesto

White fish (such as halibut, tilapia, flounder, or snapper), 4 fillets

Limes, 3, divided

Salt, ¼ teaspoon, plus additional for seasoning fish

Cilantro leaves, 1 cup

Serrano chilies, 1 to 2, stemmed, seeded, and deveined, optional

Onion, ½ medium, cut into two pieces

Pine nuts, ¼ cup

Olive oil, ¼ cup

Ground black pepper, ¼ teaspoon, or to taste

Cilantro enhances the delicious flavor of fish and seafood. Serve with rice or pasta. Almonds or walnuts can be used instead of pine nuts. —Martín

Prep Time: 15 minutes | **Total Time:** 45 minutes to 1 hour | **4 Servings**

1 Preheat the oven to 400 degrees.

2 Wash the fish and place in a dish. Squeeze the juice of one lime over the fish and sprinkle with salt. Let it marinate in the refrigerator for 10 to 15 minutes.

3 In a food processor, combine the cilantro, chilies, onion, pine nuts, the juice of the two remaining limes, olive oil, ¼ teaspoon salt, and the pepper and process until the ingredients are well mixed but not totally puréed. Pour half of the mixture in a baking dish.

4 Arrange the fish on top of the mixture. Pour the rest of the mixture over the fish.

5 Bake for 20 to 25 minutes, or until fish is solid white and flakes easily. To enhance the flavor, carefully turn the fish once during baking and brush it with the sauce.

Per Serving
Calories, 314
Total fat, 22.0 g
    Saturated fat, 2.7 g
    Trans fat, 0.0 g
    Polyunsaturated fat, 5.2 g
    Monounsaturated fat, 12.3 g
Total carbohydrate, 5 g
    Dietary fiber, 1 g
    Sugars, 2 g
Protein, 25 g
Sodium, 213 mg

vegetarian lasagna

The sweet potatoes add a wonderfully unique flavor to this delicious vegetarian lasagna. —Maya and Malena

Prep Time: 45 minutes | **Total Time:** 1 hour and 30 minutes | **10 Servings**

1 Preheat oven to 350 degrees.

2 Cook the noodles. Rinse in cold water and set aside.

3 Prepare the white sauce and set aside.

4 Cut the leeks lengthwise and wash thoroughly in a sink full of clean water to remove any grit. Chop them into small pieces. If using frozen spinach, thaw and drain well. If using fresh spinach, rinse well and chop.

5 Melt the butter in a large pan. Add the leeks, garlic, salt, pepper, and basil and sauté on medium heat for 3 minutes, or until soft. Add the spinach and cook until heated through and fragrant, several minutes. If using fresh spinach, sauté until wilted. Remove from heat and set aside.

6 In a medium bowl, mix the mozzarella and cottage cheese. Spray a 9-by-13-inch baking dish with nonstick cooking spray. Place a layer of lasagna noodles in the dish. Top with a thin layer of sweet potatoes, followed by half of the leek and spinach mixture. Top with ⅓ cup of the white sauce and one-third of the mozzarella and cottage cheese.

7 Add a second layer of noodles, another thin layer of sweet potatoes, the remaining leek and spinach mixture, ⅓ cup of the white sauce, and another layer of the mozzarella and cottage cheese. Top with a final layer of noodles. Cover with the remaining sweet potatoes, white sauce, and mozzarella and cottage cheese. Top with the Swiss cheese.

8 Cover with foil and bake for 30 to 35 minutes or until the lasagna is bubbly and the sweet potatoes are tender. Remove the foil and bake 10 more minutes, or until slightly golden.

Lasagna noodles, 1 (8-ounce) package

White Sauce (page 17), 1 cup

Leeks, 1 pound

Frozen chopped spinach, 2 (10-ounce) packages, or 2 bunches fresh spinach

Butter, 2 tablespoons

Garlic, 2 cloves, minced

Salt, ¼ teaspoon

Ground black pepper, ⅛ teaspoon

Dried basil, 1 teaspoon, or 1 tablespoon finely chopped fresh basil

Reduced-fat mozzarella cheese, shredded, 2 cups

Reduced-fat cottage cheese, 2 cups

Sweet potatoes or yams, 2 large, peeled and very thinly sliced

Swiss cheese, 6 slices

Per Serving
Calories, 369
Total fat, 15.8 g
    Saturated fat, 9.3 g
    Trans fat, 0.3 g
    Polyunsaturated fat, 1.0 g
    Monounsaturated fat, 3.5 g
Total carbohydrate, 37 g
    Dietary fiber, 4 g
    Sugars, 9 g
Protein, 22 g
Sodium, 615 mg

tilapia with mango and pineapple salsa

This dish can be made with any white fish. It's an exquisite dish to serve to guests. —Maya

Prep Time: 15 minutes | **Total Time:** 45 minutes to 1 hour | **6 Servings**

1 Season tilapia fillets with sea salt, pepper, cumin, and the juice of one lime. Marinate for about 30 minutes in refrigerator.

2 To prepare the mango salsa, place the mango, pineapple, red onion, cilantro, olive oil, rice vinegar, ginger, and the juice of the remaining lime in a glass bowl and mix thoroughly. Set aside.

3 Season the bell peppers and zucchini with salt and pepper. Spray a skillet with nonstick cooking spray and sauté the vegetables. Do not let the vegetables burn, as they can become bitter.

4 Coat a separate skillet with nonstick cooking spray and cook the fish fillets over high heat for approximately 5 to 7 minutes, turning halfway through.

5 Serve the fish topped with the mango and pineapple salsa and accompanied with the vegetables.

Tilapia or other white fish, 6 fillets

Sea salt and ground black pepper

Ground cumin, ¼ teaspoon

Limes, 2, divided

Mangoes, 2, peeled, pitted, and cubed

Pineapple, 2 slices, cubed

Red onion, finely chopped, ½ cup

Cilantro leaves, chopped, ⅓ cup

Olive oil, 1 tablespoon

Rice vinegar, 2 tablespoons

Minced ginger, 1 teaspoon

Red bell pepper, 1, stemmed, seeded, and sliced into rings

Green bell pepper, 1, stemmed, seeded, and sliced into rings

Yellow bell pepper, 1, stemmed, seeded, and sliced into rings

Zucchini, sliced, 1 cup

Per Serving
Calories, 220
Total fat, 5.0 g
    Saturated fat, 1.2 g
    Trans fat, 0.0 g
    Polyunsaturated fat, 1.1 g
    Monounsaturated fat, 4.2 g
Total carbohydrate, 23 g
    Dietary fiber, 3 g
    Sugars, 17 g
Protein, 24 g
Sodium, 56 mg

spicy seafood

Medium shrimp, 1 cup, shells still on (about ½ pound)

Water, 1½ cups

Salt, ¼ teaspoon, plus additional for salting water, divided

Red onion, 1, finely chopped

Garlic, 1 clove, minced

Ground cumin, ¼ teaspoon

Ground black pepper, ¼ teaspoon

Cayenne pepper, to taste, optional

Tomato, 1 large, peeled and diced

Roasted red peppers, chopped, ¾ cup

Canola oil, 1 tablespoon

Frozen squid (calamari), 1 cup (about ½ pound), thawed and sliced in rings

White wine, ¼ cup

Cornstarch or flour, 1 tablespoon, optional

Parmesan cheese, grated, 3 to 4 tablespoons

For the best flavor, buy a white wine you would drink instead of cooking wine.

Per Serving
Calories, 108
Total fat, 4.0 g
    Saturated fat, 0.8 g
    Trans fat, 0.0 g
    Polyunsaturated fat, 1.0 g
    Monounsaturated fat, 1.9 g
Total carbohydrate, 6 g
    Dietary fiber, 1 g
    Sugars, 3 g
Protein, 11 g
Sodium, 207 mg

In Spanish, this dish is called "Picante de mariscos," or spicy seafood. This version is quite mild, however, unless you add the cayenne pepper. Serve this dish with rice or sliced cooked potatoes and garnish with a sliced hard-boiled egg. This is one of my favorite Peruvian dishes—every time I visit my Peru, I make a point of tasting it at local Creole restaurants. —Maya

Prep Time: 30 minutes | **Total Time:** 45 minutes | **6 Servings**

1. Peel and devein the shrimp, reserving the tails and shells. Bring 1½ cups salted water to a boil. Add the tails and shells and cook for 5 minutes. Strain the broth and set aside.

2. Coat a large, heavy skillet with nonstick cooking spray and sauté the onion over medium-high heat until translucent. Add garlic, cumin, ¼ teaspoon of the salt, black pepper, and a pinch of cayenne. Sauté for 3 minutes. Add the tomato and the roasted red peppers. Cook over medium heat for 5 minutes. Add ½ cup of the shrimp broth.

3. Transfer the mixture to a blender and blend thoroughly. Taste and add more cayenne, if desired.

4. Heat the canola oil in the same skillet and sauté the shrimp and squid for several minutes, or until the shrimp are pink. Return the tomato mixture to the skillet. Add the wine and cook for 5 minutes over medium heat.

5. If the mixture is too dry, add additional shrimp broth gradually. If it is too runny, add cornstarch or flour and let cook for about 3 extra minutes, stirring constantly, until it thickens. Sprinkle with Parmesan cheese to serve.

vegetarian tamales

These tamales are delicious. Panela cheese can be found in many supermarkets, not just Hispanic markets. —Malena and Martín

Prep Time: 1 hour | **Total Time:** 2 hours | **10 Servings** (one tamale each)

1 Bring water to a boil in a 5-quart pot on the stovetop. Turn off the heat and add the corn husks. Soak until soft, about 15 minutes. Remove the husks and dry with paper towels.

2 Roast the chilies according to the instructions on page 6. Remove stems, seeds, and membranes, and cut into long strips.

3 Combine the corn masa, baking powder, and salt in a bowl and mix well. Slowly add the warm vegetable broth. Blend the masa with your hands until well combined.

4 In a large bowl, use an electric mixer to beat the softened butter for 2 minutes. Add the masa mixture and blend on low speed to get a uniform consistency.

5 Take two corn husks and place one on top of the other. If the corn husks are on the small side, place the second husk a little lower to make it easier to fold the tamale.

6 Place 2 to 3 tablespoons of the masa mixture in the center of the husk and spread it evenly into an area about 4 to 5 inches long. Leave about 2 inches of empty space on each side of the masa. Place a few slices of chili on top of the masa and top with a few slices of cheese and about a tablespoon of green salsa. Close the tamales by folding the long sides of the corn husks to the center to cover the masa mixture. Fold the short ends of the husk in and press with your fingers to secure. If needed, you can use cooking twine to tie the tamales.

7 In a large tamale pot or steamer pot, add water and bring to a boil. Place the tamales upright in the steamer, making sure the water does not touch the basket or the tamales. Cover and let tamales steam for 1 hour, checking the water level frequently and adding more when needed. After an hour, remove one tamale and let cool for a minute or two before opening the husk. The tamales are done when the dough is smooth and comes away easily from the husk.

Dried corn husks, 20 to 30 (sold in bags in Hispanic markets)

Poblano chilies, 3

Corn masa flour (such as Maseca), 2 cups

Baking powder, 1 teaspoon

Salt, ½ teaspoon

Fat-free low-sodium vegetable broth, 2 cups, warmed

Unsalted butter, 1 stick plus 3 tablespoons, softened

Panela cheese, 4 ounces, cut into thin strips

Mexican-Style Green Salsa (page 12), 1 cup, or 1 small can salsa verde

Per Serving
Calories, 240
Total fat, 15.3 g
  Saturated fat, 9.1 g
  Trans fat, 0.0 g
  Polyunsaturated fat, 1.0 g
  Monounsaturated fat, 4.0 g
Total carbohydrate, 23 g
  Dietary fiber, 3 g
  Sugars, 2 g
Protein, 4 g
Sodium, 234 mg

tasty chicken and rice from panama

Bone-in chicken breasts, 2 (about 1 pound), skin and fat removed

Garlic, 4 cloves, divided

Onion, 1, chopped, divided

Salt, to taste

Olive oil, 1 tablespoon

Tomatoes, 2 small, chopped

Carrots, shredded, 1 cup

Green bell pepper, ½, stemmed, seeded, and finely chopped

Tomato paste or ketchup, 3 tablespoons

Long grain brown rice, uncooked, 2 cups, rinsed and drained

Reduced-sodium chicken broth, 4 cups

Annatto seasoning, 1 tablespoon, or ½ tablespoon annatto paste

Pimento-stuffed green olives, 12, drained

Capers, drained, 2 tablespoons

Bay leaf, 1

Cilantro leaves, chopped, 1 tablespoon

Dried oregano, 1 teaspoon

Ground black pepper, to taste

Frozen green peas, ½ cup, or 1 small (8-ounce) can, drained

Per Serving
Calories, 284
Total fat, 5.1 g
    Saturated fat, 1.0 g
    Trans fat, 0.0 g
    Polyunsaturated fat, 1.0 g
    Monounsaturated fat, 2.7 g
Total carbohydrate, 44 g
    Dietary fiber, 4 g
    Sugars, 4 g
Protein, 16 g
Sodium, 744 mg

In Latin America, there are a lot of recipes for chicken and rice. This healthy version is from my home country. If you have my sofrito on hand (page 11), use 4 tablespoons and omit the green bell pepper and cilantro. Annatto seasoning is available in Hispanic markets in powder form or as a paste in a tube. For a quick and easy version of this recipe, you can shred a store-bought rotisserie chicken. —Malena

Prep Time: 30 minutes | **Total Time:** 1 hour and 30 minutes | **8 Servings**

1 Place chicken breasts in a pot with water to cover. Chop two cloves of the garlic and add to chicken. Add half of the onion and a pinch of salt. Bring to a boil, reduce heat to low, and simmer, uncovered, for 30 minutes, or until cooked. Turn off heat and remove the chicken. Let cool and shred by hand, discarding the bones. Reserve cooking liquid to combine with broth, if needed.

2 Chop the remaining two cloves garlic. Heat the olive oil in a large, deep skillet over medium-high heat and sauté the remaining chopped onion, garlic, tomatoes, carrots, and green bell pepper for 2 minutes, or until softened.

3 Add the shredded chicken and tomato paste and cook for 2 minutes. Add the rice and cook, stirring constantly, for 1 to 2 minutes. Add the chicken broth, annatto seasoning, olives, capers, bay leaf, cilantro, and oregano and stir to combine. Cook for 2 minutes. Taste and add salt and pepper if necessary.

4 Bring to a boil and cook over medium heat, uncovered, for 25 minutes, or until the water is reduced to the same level as the rice. Add the green peas on top of the rice without stirring. Cover and let cook for an additional 30 minutes on low, or until the rice is tender. Leave the pan covered until ready to serve. To serve, remove the bay leaf and stir to combine.

roast turkey

Turkey, 1 (15-pound)

Bitter orange juice, 2 cups, or 1½ cups 100 percent orange juice mixed with the juice of 3 limes

Unsalted butter, 4 tablespoons (½ stick), softened

Dried oregano, 1 tablespoon

Dried rosemary, 2 teaspoons, optional

Dried thyme, 2 teaspoons, optional

Flat leaf parsley, chopped, 2 teaspoons, or 1 teaspoon dried parsley, optional

Garlic, minced, 1 tablespoon

Paprika, 1 teaspoon

Sea salt, 1 teaspoon

Ground black pepper, ½ teaspoon

Onion powder, 1 teaspoon, optional

This recipe uses a classic Latin American marinade for turkey: bitter orange juice, which can be found in many supermarkets or Hispanic groceries.

Per Serving
Calories, 534
Total fat, 27.8 g
    Saturated fat, 10.1 g
    Trans fat, 0.2 g
    Polyunsaturated fat, 5.8 g
    Monounsaturated fat, 8.7 g
Total carbohydrate, 4 g
    Dietary fiber, 0 g
    Sugars, 2 g
Protein, 64 g
Sodium, 350 mg

Although Americans traditionally serve roast turkey for Thanksgiving dinner, many Latin Americans prepare it as a traditional part of Christmas Eve dinner. Cooking time will vary depending on the size of your turkey—follow the instructions on the package. When roasting poultry, it is helpful to use a meat thermometer. To do so, insert the thermometer or probe into the inner thigh near the breast, being careful not to touch any bones. The turkey is cooked when the internal temperature registers 180 degrees.

Serve the turkey with gravy (see next page), mashed potatoes or sweet potato purée, Classic Waldorf Salad (page 83), or applesauce with slices of pineapple.
—Maya and Malena

Prep Time: 15 minutes | **Total Time:** 3 to 5 hours | **16 Servings** (for a 15-pound turkey)

1 Wash the inside and outside of the turkey and dry thoroughly with paper towels. Place the turkey in a roasting pan and set aside for 15 minutes.

2 Carefully pierce the turkey with a knife in several places, taking care not to rip the skin. Douse the turkey with the bitter orange juice, using your fingers to work the marinade under the skin and into the incisions in the turkey.

3 Mix the remaining ingredients in a bowl and rub into the turkey. Carefully rub some of the mixture under the skin of the turkey, making sure not to remove the skin. Cover the turkey with plastic wrap. Let it marinate in the refrigerator for at least 3 hours, or overnight.

4 When ready to cook, preheat the oven to 350 degrees. Discard the plastic wrap and marinade, and cover the turkey with aluminum foil. Roast the turkey depending on its weight, according to package instructions. Every 30 minutes or so during cooking, baste the turkey with the liquid in the pan.

5 Approximately 20 minutes before the turkey is finished roasting, remove the aluminum foil to allow the skin to brown. Continue basting periodically. When the interior of the turkey has reached 180 degrees, remove from the oven and let stand for 10 to 15 minutes before carving.

roast turkey gravy

Serve our scrumptious roast turkey with this flavorful homemade gravy.
—Malena

Reduced-sodium chicken broth or water, 3 cups

Remaining drippings from the roasting pan, 6 tablespoons minimum

All-purpose flour, 4 tablespoons

Salt, ¼ teaspoon

Ground black pepper, ⅛ teaspoon

Prep Time: 10 minutes | **Total Time:** 1 hour and 30 minutes | **6 Servings** (about ⅓ cup each)

1 When the turkey has finished roasting, warm the chicken broth over medium-low heat.

2 In a separate saucepan, measure about 4 tablespoons of the drippings from the roasting pan and place over medium-high heat. Add the flour and cook, stirring constantly with a wire whisk. Once the flour starts to brown, slowly add the remaining pan drippings. Avoid using the fat. Continue to stir until the flour has thickened and it turns smooth.

3 Slowly add 2 cups of the warm chicken broth, stirring constantly. Bring to a boil, lower heat, and cook until the gravy has thickened and is bubbly, adding more broth as needed. Season with salt and pepper. Serve warm.

Per Serving
Calories, 81
Total fat, 6.0 g
    Saturated fat, 2.3 g
    Trans fat, 0.0 g
    Polyunsaturated fat, 0.6 g
    Monounsaturated fat, 2.6 g
Total carbohydrate, 5 g
    Dietary fiber, 0 g
    Sugars, 0 g
Protein, 2 g
Sodium, 407 mg

marsala chicken

To make this recipe vegetarian, use firm tofu instead of chicken. Sauté cubed tofu in butter and sprinkle with a tablespoon of brown sugar. Then add the tofu to the frying pan at the same time as the green olives, capers, and parsley. My son, Chris, who is a vegetarian, loves this dish. I've prepared it at home for him, and now it's one of the family's favorite dishes. —Maya

Prep Time: 20 minutes | **Total Time:** 1 hour and 15 minutes | **6 Servings**

1 Put the flour in a dish and add a pinch each of salt, pepper, and cayenne. Mix well. Coat each piece of chicken with the seasoned flour; shake off excess.

2 Heat the olive oil in a frying pan and brown the chicken pieces on all sides. Remove and set aside.

3 Add the onion to the same frying pan. When it starts to brown, add the oregano and just a pinch of black pepper. Add the tomatoes, wine, and chicken broth. Return the chicken to the frying pan and lower the heat. Cover and cook on low for about 45 minutes.

4 Five minutes before serving, add the green olives, capers, and parsley. Cook for an additional 5 minutes. Taste and add salt, if necessary. Serve with rice and a vegetable of your choice.

All-purpose flour, ¼ cup

Salt and ground black pepper

Cayenne pepper, to taste

Chicken drumsticks and thighs, 6 pieces, skin removed

Olive oil, 1½ tablespoons

Yellow onion, 1, cut into long thin strips

Dried or fresh oregano, 1 teaspoon

Roma tomatoes, 2, finely chopped

Marsala wine, ½ cup

Reduced-sodium chicken broth, ½ cup

Green olives, ¼ cup

Capers, drained, 1 tablespoon

Flat leaf parsley, chopped, ¼ cup

Per Serving
Calories, 177
Total fat, 8.5 g
    Saturated fat, 1.7 g
    Trans fat, 0.0 g
    Polyunsaturated fat, 1.4 g
    Monounsaturated fat, 4.6 g
Total carbohydrate, 9 g
    Dietary fiber, 1 g
    Sugars, 3 g
Protein, 14 g
Sodium, 219 mg

tuna lasagna

Lasagna noodles, 1 pound (12 noodles)

Green bell pepper, 1, stemmed, seeded, and finely chopped

Yellow onion, ½, finely chopped

Celery, 1 stalk, finely chopped

Flat leaf parsley, finely chopped, 2 tablespoons

Garlic, 1 clove, minced

Frozen mixed vegetables, 2 cups

Chunk light tuna packed in water, 2 (12-ounce) cans, drained

Tomato sauce, 1 (8-ounce) can

Green olives, pitted and sliced, ½ cup

Salt and ground black pepper, to taste

Homemade Tomato Sauce (page 16) or store-bought marinara sauce, 2 cups

Reduced-fat mozzarella cheese, shredded, 2 cups

Parmesan cheese, grated, ½ cup

This lasagna recipe is fit for a queen. The tuna is a great alternative to ground beef. Enjoy! —Malena

Prep Time: 25 minutes | **Total Time:** 1 hour and 30 minutes | **10 Servings**

1 Preheat oven to 350 degrees.

2 Cook the noodles and set aside. Rinse with cold water.

3 Coat a frying pan with nonstick cooking spray. Over medium heat, sauté the green pepper, onion, celery, parsley, and garlic for 5 minutes. Add mixed vegetables and cook for 3 minutes.

4 Add the drained tuna and the canned tomato sauce. Cook for 5 minutes. Add the olives and salt and pepper and set aside.

5 Spread ½ cup of the homemade tomato sauce in the bottom of a 9-by-13-inch baking dish. Cover the tomato sauce with a layer of noodles. Add a layer of homemade tomato sauce, followed by half of the tuna mixture and a layer of mozzarella.

6 Place a second layer of noodles on top, followed by the remaining homemade tomato sauce, the remaining tuna mixture, and the mozzarella cheese (reserving about ½ cup for the top). Cover with one more layer of noodles. Top with the remaining mozzarella cheese and the Parmesan cheese.

7 Cover with foil and bake for 35 minutes. Uncover and bake an additional 10 to 15 minutes or until cheese is melted. Let stand a few minutes before serving.

Per Serving
Calories, 352
Total fat, 7.9 g
    Saturated fat, 3.6 g
    Trans fat, 0.0 g
    Polyunsaturated fat, 1.0 g
    Monounsaturated fat, 2.0 g
Total carbohydrate, 44 g
    Dietary fiber, 4 g
    Sugars, 7 g
Protein, 27 g
Sodium, 650 mg

meatballs in chipotle sauce

I ate these spicy meatballs for the first time at a friend's house and loved them. Chipotle peppers in adobo sauce can be found in small cans in the Hispanic foods section of most supermarkets. If you have never cooked with them, start with the smallest amount and taste the sauce as you go. Serve with rice and vegetables of your choice. —Martin

Garlic, 2 cloves, divided

Ground turkey breast, 1 pound

Egg, 1

Ground cumin, 1 teaspoon

Dried mint leaves, 1½ teaspoons, or 1 tablespoon chopped fresh mint

Raisins, ⅓ cup (about one small box)

Bread crumbs, ⅓ cup

Onion, chopped, ¾ cup, divided

Canola oil, 1 tablespoon

Tomatoes, 3 to 4 large (about 1 pound), or 1 (28-ounce) can fire-roasted whole tomatoes

Reduced-sodium chicken bouillon granules, 1 tablespoon, or 1 cube reduced-sodium chicken bouillon

Chipotle peppers in adobo sauce, 1 to 2, or to taste

Water, ½ cup, optional

Prep Time: 30 minutes | **Total Time:** 1 hour | **6 Servings** (four meatballs each)

---

1 Mince one clove garlic. Combine the ground turkey breast, egg, cumin, mint, raisins, and bread crumbs with ¼ cup of the chopped onion and the minced garlic in a large bowl. Mix thoroughly. Form into medium-sized balls.

2 Heat the oil in a pan and cook the meatballs for 5 minutes, turning them during cooking to brown. Remove and set aside. (Alternatively, you can bake the meatballs at 350 degrees for 25 to 30 minutes, turning once.)

3 In a dry skillet, roast the tomatoes over medium heat, turing to cook on all sides, for 10 minutes, or until peels are soft and darkened.

4 Place the tomatoes in a blender with the remaining ½ cup onion, the remaining clove of garlic, and the chicken bouillon and blend. Add the chipotle peppers and blend. If using fresh tomatoes, add ½ cup water and blend again. Taste the sauce and add additional chipotle pepper, as desired.

5 Pour the blended sauce into a saucepan and cook over high heat for 5 minutes, or until boiling. Once the sauce starts to boil, add the meatballs, lower the heat to medium low, cover the saucepan, and cook until meatballs are completely done—about 20 to 25 minutes.

Per Serving
Calories, 196
Total fat, 5.3 g
 Saturated fat, 0.9 g
 Trans fat, 0.0 g
 Polyunsaturated fat, 1.6 g
 Monounsaturated fat, 2.4 g
Total carbohydrate, 16 g
 Dietary fiber, 2 g
 Sugars, 8 g
Protein, 22 g
Sodium, 360 mg

chicken fricassee

Chicken, 1 whole, cut into 8 pieces (2 split breasts, 2 drumsticks, 2 thighs, 2 wings)

Annatto paste, 1 tablespoon

Ground cumin, ½ teaspoon

Worcestershire sauce, 2 tablespoons

Malena's Sofrito (page 10), 2 tablespoons

Canola oil, 1 tablespoon

Onions, 2, peeled and quartered

Green bell pepper, 1, stemmed, seeded, and chopped

Cilantro leaves, ½ cup

Celery, 1 stalk, chopped (about ½ cup)

Carrots, 3, peeled and sliced

Homemade Tomato Sauce (page 16), 3½ cups, or 1 (28-ounce) can fire-roasted crushed tomatoes

This chicken dish can be baked or prepared in a slow cooker. Using the slow cooker can be a big help for busy families who want to find dinner ready when they return home from a long day. I like to serve this dish with rice and beans. My husband, Bill, does not care for cilantro, so I tend to use whole cilantro sprigs to make it easier to remove them before serving. —Malena

Prep Time: 30 minutes | **Total Time:** 2 to 3 hours (including marination) | **6 Servings**

1 If baking the chicken instead of using a slow cooker, preheat the oven to 350 degrees. Preparation is the same for both methods of cooking.

2 Wash the chicken and remove the skin and excess fat. Put the chicken pieces in a glass or Pyrex dish and add the annatto paste, cumin, Worcestershire sauce, and sofrito. Toss thoroughly to coat. Cover the chicken and let it marinate in the refrigerator for 1 to 2 hours.

3 Heat the canola oil in a skillet over medium-high heat and sauté the chicken for approximately 3 minutes on each side, until it is golden brown but not cooked through. You may need to do this step in batches.

4 Place the onions, green bell pepper, cilantro, celery, and carrots in a baking dish or slow cooker and toss to combine. Arrange the chicken over the vegetables and top with the tomato sauce.

5 If baking, cover the baking dish with aluminum foil and bake for 35 to 40 minutes, turning the chicken pieces after 25 minutes so they will cook evenly. If using the slow cooker, cook on low for 5 hours.

Per Serving
Calories, 230
Total fat, 7.1 g
   Saturated fat, 1.4 g
   Trans fat, 0.0 g
   Polyunsaturated fat, 1.8 g
   Monounsaturated fat, 3.1 g
Total carbohydrate, 18 g
   Dietary fiber, 4 g
   Sugars, 10 g
Protein, 22 g
Sodium, 600 mg

chicken rolls supreme

This recipe is good for parties and festivities, but children love it, too.
—*Martin*

Prep Time: 15 minutes | **Total Time:** 45 minutes | **4 Servings**

1 Preheat oven to 400 degrees.

2 Place the chicken breasts between two pieces of plastic wrap and pound each breast to flatten to uniform thickness. Season with salt and pepper.

3 In a bowl, combine the tomato, spinach, basil, cheese, almonds, oregano, and a pinch of black pepper and mix well. Spread about 2 tablespoons of this mixture over each chicken breast. Roll them up and secure them with toothpicks.

4 Coat a skillet with nonstick cooking spray and brown the chicken rolls on all sides. Transfer the chicken rolls to a greased baking dish.

5 Put 1 teaspoon of butter on top of each roll. Bake for 25 to 30 minutes, or until internal temperature reaches 165 degrees.

Boneless, skinless chicken breasts, 4

Salt and ground black pepper

Tomato, 1 large, seeded and finely chopped

Fresh spinach, 1 bunch, stems removed, chopped

Fresh basil leaves, 6, chopped

Parmesan cheese, shredded, ¼ cup

Slivered almonds, ¼ cup

Dried oregano, ¼ teaspoon

Butter, 4 teaspoons

Per Serving
Calories, 277
Total fat, 13.0 g
    Saturated fat, 4.7 g
    Trans fat, 0.2 g
    Polyunsaturated fat, 2.0 g
    Monounsaturated fat, 5.1 g
Total carbohydrate, 5 g
    Dietary fiber, 2 g
    Sugars, 2 g
Protein, 35 g
Sodium, 188 mg

sea and garden delight

Red or yellow onion, 1 large, peeled and julienned

Garlic, 1 clove, minced

Green bell pepper, 1, stemmed, seeded, and julienned

Red bell pepper, 1, stemmed, seeded, and julienned

Yellow bell pepper, 1, stemmed, seeded, and julienned

Tomatoes, 2 large, peeled and julienned

Salt, ½ teaspoon, divided

Firm white fish (such as tilapia or orange roughy), 3 fillets

Ground cumin, ¼ teaspoon

Lemon pepper, ½ teaspoon

Canola oil, 1 tablespoon

Small or medium shrimp, ½ pound, peeled, deveined, tails removed

Small or medium scallops, ½ pound

Juice of 1 or 2 limes

Flat leaf parsley, chopped, ¼ cup

This is a very special dish I enjoy making for my friends, and they love it! —Maya

Prep Time: 15 minutes | **Total Time:** 30 minutes | **6 Servings**

1 Coat a large frying pan with nonstick cooking spray. Over medium heat, cook the onion until golden brown. Add the garlic and bell peppers and sauté for 2 minutes. Add the tomatoes and ¼ teaspoon of the salt. Lower heat and cook for 5 minutes. Remove the vegetables from the pan and set aside.

2 Cut the fish fillets in half. Season with cumin, the remaining salt, and lemon pepper.

3 Heat the tablespoon of canola oil in the same pan over medium heat. Add the fish fillets and cook for 2 minutes, or until golden brown on first side. Turn carefully so the fillets do not fall apart, and cover them with the vegetable mixture. Let them cook for another 2 minutes, or until browned on other side.

4 Add the shrimp, scallops, and the juice of one lime. Lower heat and cook for about 5 to 7 minutes, or until the shrimp are cooked through and pink.

5 Before serving, taste and add more lime juice, if desired. Add the chopped parsley. Serve with rice. Garnish with additional parsley, if desired.

Per Serving
Calories, 179
Total fat, 4.3 g
    Saturated fat, 0.8 g
    Trans fat, 0.0 g
    Polyunsaturated fat, 1.2 g
    Monounsaturated fat, 2.0 g
Total carbohydrate, 13 g
    Dietary fiber, 3 g
    Sugars, 6 g
Protein, 24 g
Sodium, 172 mg

creamy cilantro chicken

Frozen white corn, 2½ cups, thawed, or 2 (15-ounce) cans Shoepeg white corn, drained

Cilantro leaves, ⅓ cup

Baby spinach, 1 cup

Milk (skim or 1 percent), 1 to 1½ cups, divided

Canola oil, 2 teaspoons, divided

White onion, finely chopped, ½ cup

Garlic, 1 clove, minced

Ground cumin, ½ teaspoon, divided

Salt and ground black pepper

Boneless, skinless chicken breasts, 3, cut into thin strips or bite-sized pieces

This dish suggests the flavor of cilantro tamales from Peru but without all the work. The flavor of white corn, unlike yellow corn, reminds me of corn from Peru, except the kernels are a lot smaller. I like to serve this dish with rice, garnished with slices of hard-boiled egg. —Maya

Prep Time: 15 minutes | **Total Time:** 45 minutes to 1 hour | **6 Servings**

1. Combine the corn, cilantro, spinach, and 1 cup of the milk in a food processor or blender and blend well. This step may have to be done in batches.

2. Heat 1 teaspoon of the canola oil in a large skillet and sauté the chopped onion. When the onion is translucent, add the garlic. Season with ¼ teaspoon of the cumin and a pinch of salt and pepper. Sauté for 5 minutes.

3. Pour the corn mixture into the skillet and cook over medium heat, stirring frequently, for 5 to 10 minutes, or until it starts bubbling. If the mixture is too thick, add ¼ to ½ cup milk. Lower the heat and simmer for 5 minutes.

4. Season the chicken with the other ¼ teaspoon ground cumin, salt, and pepper. In another skillet, heat the remaining teaspoon of canola oil and sauté the chicken until it is golden brown and cooked through.

5. Transfer the cooked chicken to the skillet with the corn mixture and simmer for an additional 5 to 7 minutes.

Per Serving
Calories, 178
Total fat, 3.9 g
    Saturated fat, 0.7 g
    Trans fat, 0.0 g
    Polyunsaturated fat, 1.1 g
    Monounsaturated fat, 1.7 g
Total carbohydrate, 18 g
    Dietary fiber, 2 g
    Sugars, 5 g
Protein, 19 g
Sodium, 64 mg

exotic seafood rice

The secret ingredient for this dish is annatto, a mild spice used often in Latin American cooking. It is available in Hispanic markets in powder form or as a paste in a tube. Saffron can also be used, although it is more expensive. —Malena

Prep Time: 15 minutes | **Total Time:** 1 hour | **6 Servings**

1 Defrost the seafood mix and place in a glass dish. Add the shrimp and sprinkle with 2 tablespoons of sofrito and a pinch of salt and pepper. Toss to combine. Refrigerate the seafood while you prepare the rest of the ingredients.

2 Heat olive oil over medium-high heat in a 5-quart pot. Sauté the onion, green pepper, garlic, celery, and green onions for about 5 minutes, or until tender, stirring frequently. Add the rice and mix well. Add the seafood.

3 Add 4½ cups water to the pot and stir for 1 minute. Bring to a boil. When the mixture begins to boil, add the annatto seasoning and the cilantro. Stir to combine and cook for 1 minute. Taste the broth and add salt and pepper if necessary.

4 Reduce heat to medium and cook for 25 minutes, or until the water has reduced to the same level as the rice. Place the peas and carrots and olives on top, without stirring the rice. Cover and cook over low heat for an additional 30 minutes, or until the rice is fully cooked.

5 Leave the pot covered until ready to serve. When ready to serve, stir to combine.

Frozen seafood mix (with imitation crabmeat, octopus, squid, and shrimp), 1 pound

Small fresh or frozen shrimp, ½ pound, peeled, deveined, tails removed

Malena's Sofrito (page 11), 2 tablespoons, optional

Salt and ground black pepper

Olive oil, 1 tablespoon

Onion, ½, chopped

Green bell pepper, 1, stemmed, seeded, and finely chopped

Garlic, 1 clove, minced

Celery, 1 stalk, finely chopped

Green onions, 3, thinly sliced

Long grain brown rice, uncooked, 2 cups, rinsed and drained

Water, 4½ cups

Annatto seasoning or dried saffron, 1 tablespoon

Cilantro leaves, chopped, 2 tablespoons

Frozen peas and carrots, 1 cup, or 1 small (8.5-ounce) can, drained

Stuffed green olives, ⅓ cup, sliced

Per Serving
Calories, 352
Total fat, 6.3 g
  Saturated fat, 1.0 g
  Trans fat, 0.0 g
  Polyunsaturated fat, 1.4 g
  Monounsaturated fat, 3.2 g
Total carbohydrate, 55 g
  Dietary fiber, 5 g
  Sugars, 5 g
Protein, 18 g
Sodium, 655 mg

manoli's mouthwatering eggplant

Eggplant, 1 large

Salt, 2 teaspoons, divided

Ground black pepper, 1 teaspoon, divided

Dried oregano, 1 teaspoon

Extra-virgin olive oil, 4 tablespoons, divided

Garlic, 3 cloves, sliced thinly

Balsamic vinegar, 1 teaspoon

Freshly squeezed lime juice, ⅓ cup

Roasted red pepper, sliced, 1 tablespoon

Flat leaf parsley, chopped, 2 tablespoons

My friend Chef Emmanuel "Manoli" Kalormakis was passionate about Greek and Italian cuisine. I visited him in Panama at the beginning of 2009. One Saturday evening during my visit, we sat down to talk about Panamanian cuisine, eggplant, and other vegetables that I should include in this cookbook. He taught me how to make this dish during my visit. Sadly, Chef Manoli passed away just two weeks later, but he left behind this recipe as a gift. Manoli, you'll be remembered for all the delicious dishes you served in your restaurants, and we publish this recipe here to honor you. Farewell, Manoli! —Malena

Prep Time: 15 minutes | **Total Time:** 30 minutes | **6 Servings**

1 Preheat oven to 350 degrees.

2 Peel the eggplant and slice lengthwise into ¼-inch-thick slices. Place the eggplant in a bowl of saltwater to cover. Let soak for 5 minutes. Remove from the water, rinse, and drain. Place in a baking dish.

3 Sprinkle the eggplant with 1 teaspoon of the salt, ½ teaspoon of the black pepper, and the oregano. Drizzle with 2 tablespoons of the olive oil and top with the sliced garlic. Bake for 15 to 20 minutes, or until the eggplant is dry.

4 While the eggplant is cooking, combine the balsamic vinegar, lime juice, the remaining olive oil, and the remaining salt and pepper in a glass serving dish.

5 Remove the eggplant from the oven. Cut each slice into four to six strips lengthwise and place in the serving dish with the vinegar mixture. Toss to coat. Garnish with sliced roasted red pepper and chopped parsley and serve.

Per Serving
Calories, 125
Total fat, 9.3 g
    Saturated fat, 1.3 g
    Trans fat, 0.0 g
    Polyunsaturated fat, 1.1 g
    Monounsaturated fat, 6.6 g
Total carbohydrate, 11 g
    Dietary fiber, 3 g
    Sugars, 4 g
Protein, 1 g
Sodium, 794 mg

desserts

ricotta crème with berries

This recipe calls for agave nectar (sometimes called agave syrup), an organic sweetener. If you can't find it, substitute honey instead. If using strawberries, hull and halve the berries before mixing with the sugar and lime juice. —Maya

Prep Time: 15 minutes | **Total Time:** 1 hour and 15 minutes | **6 Servings**

1 Put the berries in a glass bowl with the sugar and the juice of half a lime. Stir gently to combine. Refrigerate for 1 hour to release the natural juices.

2 Mix the ricotta cheese, vanilla extract, and agave nectar in a separate bowl. Refrigerate the ricotta mixture to chill.

3 To serve, sprinkle a large spoonful of the berry mixture on top of a couple of scoops of the chilled ricotta mixture.

Fresh berries, 1 cup (such as strawberries, raspberries, or blackberries)

Raw sugar or light brown sugar, 1 teaspoon

Juice of ½ lime or lemon

Part-skim ricotta cheese, 3 cups

Vanilla extract, ¼ teaspoon

Agave nectar, 3 tablespoons

Per Serving
Calories, 206
Total fat, 9.8 g
    Saturated fat, 6.1 g
    Trans fat, 0.0 g
    Polyunsaturated fat, 0.4 g
    Monounsaturated fat, 2.9 g
Total carbohydrate, 16 g
    Dietary fiber, 1 g
    Sugars, 8 g
Protein, 14 g
Sodium, 160 mg

fruit and ginger macedonia

Orange, 1, peeled and segmented

Grapefruit, 1, peeled and segmented

Mango, 1, peeled, pitted, and chopped into bite-sized pieces

Apple, 1, cored and cut into bite-sized pieces

Pear, 1, peeled, cored, and cut into bite-sized pieces

Peach, 1, peeled, pitted, and cut into bite-sized pieces

Strawberries, 1 cup, hulled and halved

Orange juice, 1 cup

Light brown sugar, 2 tablespoons

Ground ginger, 1 teaspoon

Low-fat natural or plain yogurt, 1 cup

This Mediterranean-inspired fruit salad is delicious and unusual. Segmenting an orange (or other citrus fruit) is easy. First, cut off the top and bottom of the orange. Hold the orange in your hand and slice off the skin and pith in strips from top to bottom. Once all the skin is gone, use your knife to carefully separate the orange wedges from the membranes.
—*Malena*

Prep Time: 30 minutes | **Total Time:** 45 minutes to 1 hour | **6 Servings**

1 Combine the orange, grapefruit, mango, apple, pear, peach, and strawberries in a large bowl.

2 In a separate container, combine the orange juice, brown sugar, and ground ginger. Mix well and pour onto the fruit.

3 Let this mixture sit in the refrigerator for 15 minutes or until time to serve.

4 When ready to serve, stir in the yogurt and mix well.

Per Serving
Calories, 161
Total fat, 1.1 g
  Saturated fat, 0.5 g
  Trans fat, 0.0 g
  Polyunsaturated fat, 0.2 g
  Monounsaturated fat, 0.3 g
Total carbohydrate, 37 g
  Dietary fiber, 4 g
  Sugars, 30 g
Protein, 4 g
Sodium, 31 mg

rice pudding

This easy rice pudding recipe is delicious, economical, and can be prepared the day before. —Maya

Prep Time: 15 minutes | **Total Time:** 1 hour and 15 minutes | **10 Servings**

1 Put the rice in a colander and wash thoroughly until the water is clear.

2 Place the rice in a pot with a heavy bottom, along with 4 cups of water, the cinnamon stick, cloves, star anise, and the lemon peel.

3 Bring to a boil over medium-high heat and cook, partially covered, for 15 to 20 minutes, without stirring, until the rice is almost cooked. Remove the lemon peel and cinnamon stick.

4 Add the milk and reduce heat to medium-low. Cook for 15 minutes, or until the rice is completely cooked, stirring frequently with a wooden spoon to prevent the rice from sticking and burning. Test the rice for doneness. Remove the cloves and star anise.

5 Add the raisins, sweetened condensed milk, coconut flakes, and walnuts. Cook for an additional 15 minutes over low heat, or until the mixture thickens, stirring frequently. Add the vanilla, salt, and rum and cook for 5 minutes. Taste the rice and add sugar, if necessary. If you add more sugar, continue to cook over low heat for about 5 more minutes. Remove from heat and allow to cool.

6 Serve at room temperature or chilled in small glass bowls, sprinkled with ground cinnamon.

Medium or short grain white rice, uncooked, 2 cups

Water, 4 cups

Cinnamon, 1 stick

Cloves, 5

Star anise, 3 pods, optional

Peel of 1 lemon

Milk (1 percent), 4 cups

Raisins, ½ cup

Fat-free sweetened condensed milk, 1 (14-ounce) can

Unsweetened coconut flakes, ½ cup

Walnuts or slivered almonds, chopped, ¼ cup

Vanilla extract, 1 tablespoon

Salt, ½ teaspoon

Rum or any fruit liqueur, 2 tablespoons, optional

Sugar, ½ cup, optional

Ground cinnamon, 1 teaspoon

Per Serving
Calories, 214
Total fat, 2.9 g
   Saturated fat, 1.6 g
   Trans fat, 0.0 g
   Polyunsaturated fat, 0.7 g
   Monounsaturated fat, 0.3 g
Total carbohydrate, 42 g
   Dietary fiber, 1 g
   Sugars, 24 g
Protein, 6 g
Sodium, 114 mg

fiesta strawberries

Sugar, ¼ cup

Orange juice, ⅓ cup

Fresh strawberries, sliced, 2 cups

Cognac with orange essence, ⅓ cup

Ground green peppercorn, ½ teaspoon

Nonfat vanilla or lemon frozen yogurt, 1 pint

Fresh mint

This dessert is perfect for special occasions. —Martín

Prep Time: 10 minutes | **Total Time:** 15 minutes | **6 Servings**

1 Put the sugar in a pan over medium heat. Add the orange juice and stir the mixture until it reaches a boil.

2 Add the strawberries to the pan and cook for a few moments to warm.

3 Pour Cognac over the strawberries and let it cook for about 3 minutes.

4 Add green peppercorn and mix carefully.

5 Scoop ⅓ cup frozen yogurt into a glass bowl and cover with the strawberry mixture. Garnish with a mint leaf.

Per Serving
Calories, 147
Total fat, 0.2 g
    Saturated fat, 0.0 g
    Trans fat, 0.0 g
    Polyunsaturated fat, 0.1 g
    Monounsaturated fat, 0.0 g
Total carbohydrate, 27 g
    Dietary fiber, 1 g
    Sugars, 24 g
Protein, 3 g
Sodium, 41 mg

dulce de leche crepes

Flour tortillas, 8 small

Dulce de leche, 1 cup

Walnuts, finely chopped, ½ cup

Bananas, 3, thinly sliced

I devised these crepes for a food event sponsored by a brand of flour tortillas. My challenge was to prepare a new and tasty dish to entice the audience. It occurred to me to make a recipe using the caramel spread called "dulce de leche" or "cajeta," which can be found in cans in the Hispanic foods section in most supermarkets. We already had bananas on hand, and the combination of the two ingredients was an immense crowd pleaser. Mission accomplished! —Martín

Prep Time: 5 minutes | **Total Time:** 20 minutes | **8 Servings**

1 Spray a skillet with nonstick cooking spray and place over medium-high heat. Cook the tortillas one at a time until softened and lightly browned on both sides.

2 While tortillas are still warm, apply 2 tablespoons of dulce de leche to each tortilla. Top with chopped nuts and place banana slices on one half of the tortilla. Fold in half and serve.

Per Serving
Calories, 304
Total fat, 11.2 g
   Saturated fat, 2.7 g
   Trans fat, 0.1 g
   Polyunsaturated fat, 4.2 g
   Monounsaturated fat, 2.6 g
Total carbohydrate, 48 g
   Dietary fiber, 3 g
   Sugars, 27 g
Protein, 5 g
Sodium, 284 mg

brazilian mousse

This recipe was given to me by my friend Cristina Silva from Brazil. She told me it is a common and beloved dessert in Brazil. Passion fruit in Spanish is "maracuyá." If you cannot find frozen passion fruit juice for this recipe, use freshly squeezed orange juice instead. You can add a teaspoon of vanilla extract for a slightly different flavor.

Since this recipe contains uncooked egg whites, be sure to use pasteurized eggs. —Maya

Low-fat sweetened condensed milk, 1 (13-ounce) can

Frozen passion fruit concentrate, 1 cup

Egg whites, 3

Unflavored gelatin (such as Knox), 1 envelope

Prep Time: 30 minutes | **Total Time:** 6 hours and 30 minutes (including refrigeration) | **8 Servings**

1 Put the condensed milk and passion fruit concentrate into a blender and purée.

2 With a mixer or whisk, beat egg whites until stiff. Gently fold into the milk and fruit mixture.

3 Following the package instructions, dissolve the gelatin. Add to the mixture.

4 Rinse a ring mold with very cold water and pour the mixture into it. Alternatively, you can pour it into individual glass dishes. Refrigerate for 6 hours.

5 To serve, unmold the mousse onto a round large plate or serve in the individual glass dishes.

Per Serving
Calories, 214
Total fat, 2.5 g
    Saturated fat, 1.6 g
    Trans fat, 0.0 g
    Polyunsaturated fat, 0.0 g
    Monounsaturated fat, 0.7 g
Total carbohydrate, 39 g
    Dietary fiber, 0 g
    Sugars, 38 g
Protein, 8 g
Sodium, 88 mg

easy cuatro leches cake

Ladyfinger cookies, 48

Dulce de leche, ½ to ¾ cup

Low-fat sweetened condensed milk, 1 cup

Light whipping cream, 1 cup

Fat-free evaporated milk, 1 cup

Fresh berries (sliced strawberries, blueberries, and raspberries), 3 cups

This dessert is ideal for parties and special occasions. This recipe is a simple and fast version of the traditional tres leches cake (cake with three milks). Dulce de leche is a caramel spread popular in many Latin American countries and is available in the Hispanic foods section of most supermarkets. —Malena

Prep Time: 30 minutes | **Total Time:** 8 hours (including refrigeration) | **12 Servings**

1 Place a layer of ladyfingers at the bottom of an 11-by-8-inch Pyrex or glass baking dish.

2 In the microwave or on the stovetop, heat the dulce de leche slightly until it is soft and easy to spread. Use a spatula to spread a thin layer of dulce de leche on top of the ladyfingers. Place another layer of ladyfingers on top of the dulce de leche. Poke several holes in each cookie with a toothpick.

3 Place the baking dish in the freezer for 20 to 30 minutes so the dulce de leche can harden.

4 Once the dulce de leche has hardened, remove the dish from freezer. Put the sweetened condensed milk, whipping cream, and evaporated milk in a blender and mix well for 1 to 2 minutes. Pour the milk mixture over the ladyfingers.

5 Refrigerate overnight and serve the following day. Top with berries before serving.

To reduce the calories, this version with four milks uses reduced-fat milks and eliminates the frosting on top. If you can find them, use fresh ladyfingers, which may be available in your supermarket's bakery.

Per Serving
Calories, 372
Total fat, 12.6 g
  Saturated fat, 6.6 g
  Trans fat, 0.0 g
  Polyunsaturated fat, 1.0 g
  Monounsaturated fat, 4.2 g
Total carbohydrate, 56 g
  Dietary fiber, 2 g
  Sugars, 51 g
Protein, 9 g
Sodium, 154 mg

how to stock your kitchen to promote healthy eating

Stock your kitchen and pantry with a variety of healthful foods. Keeping these flavorful ingredients on hand can help you create satisfying meals with ease on those busy nights when the last thing you want to do is stop at the grocery store.

In the Cupboard

- Canned beans, such as black beans, chickpeas, cannellini beans, pinto beans, kidney beans, black-eyed peas, and refried beans (not cooked in lard)
- Grains, such as brown rice, long grain rice, quinoa, and barley
- Pasta (whole wheat or white), such as penne, bowties, couscous, egg noodles, lasagna noodles, fettuccine, and spinach noodles
- Pretzels, whole wheat crackers, breadsticks, dry cereals, and granola
- Hot cereals, such as oatmeal (quick-cooking and rolled oats) and Cream of Wheat
- Flour, cornmeal, bread crumbs
- Onions, potatoes, garlic
- Canned tomatoes (diced or whole), tomato sauce, tomato paste, salsa, pizza and pasta sauces, and ketchup
- Canned fruits in juice, such as pineapple, pears, mandarin oranges, and peaches
- Chipotle peppers in adobo sauce
- Canned or jarred jalapeño peppers
- Roasted red peppers
- Applesauce (without added sugar)
- Dried fruits, such as raisins, sweetened cranberries, apricots, prunes, and blueberries
- Reduced-sodium broths
- Canned meats, such as tuna, salmon, and chicken, packed in water
- Peanut butter (all-natural or regular)
- Nuts, such as almonds (whole and slivered), walnuts, sunflower seeds, and pine nuts
- Evaporated milk (low-fat)
- Red wine vinegar, white wine vinegar, rice vinegar
- Oils, including olive oil, canola oil, and nonfat cooking spray
- Sweeteners, such as honey, agave nectar, and light brown sugar
- Spices, such as cumin, chili powder, cayenne pepper, dried oregano and basil, annatto paste, lemon pepper, garlic powder, kosher salt, white pepper, and dried mint

In the Refrigerator

- In-season vegetables and fruits
- Reduced-fat milk and buttermilk or lactose-free milk
- Reduced-fat or nonfat yogurt (without added sugar) and Greek yogurt
- Reduced-fat or regular cheeses, such as Cheddar, mozzarella, feta, Monterey jack, Parmesan, ricotta, cottage cheese, queso fresco, and oaxaca
- Reduced-fat sour cream, cream cheese, and crema Mexicana
- Whole wheat flour or corn tortillas
- Eggs
- Minced garlic
- Sauces: Worcestershire sauce, reduced-sodium soy sauce, and hot sauce
- Salad dressing and condiments, Dijon mustard
- 100 percent fruit and vegetable juices
- Hummus

In the Freezer

- Frozen vegetables, fruits, and canned juice concentrates (100 percent juice)
- Frozen chopped onions and chopped green peppers
- Breads, such as whole grain breads, dinner rolls, English muffins, bagels, and pita bread
- Lean meats, such as chicken breast, ground turkey breast, and extra lean ground beef
- Seafood, such as salmon, flounder, tilapia, red snapper, shrimp, and scallops

recipe makeovers 101:
three steps to healthier meals

If food doesn't taste good, it won't be eaten—it's as simple as that. Fortunately, there are many ways to cut down on the calories you don't want without sacrificing flavor. It's also easy to add extra nutrients by adding more fruits, vegetables, and whole grains. Use the tips below to achieve great taste—with a lot fewer calories—in your own recipes.

Step 1: Increase the vegetables, fruits, and whole grains.

- Start your day by making fruit smoothies for the entire family.
- Add fresh or dried fruits, such as banana slices, blueberries, or raisins to your cereal instead of sugar.
- Eat one salad a day.
- Add fresh or dried fruits, such as chopped apples, raisins, prunes, kiwi, or orange sections to green leafy salads instead of high-calorie salad dressings.
- Add dried fruits or frozen vegetables, such as peas and carrots, to rice, quinoa, or other grain-based dishes.
- Add chopped carrots, broccoli, or a mix of your favorite vegetables to soups, salads, and casseroles.
- Add your favorite canned beans to soups, stews, and salads. However, drain the beans and rinse with water to reduce the sodium content.
- Substitute whole wheat flour for up to half (or more) of the white flour called for in a recipe.
- Add ¼ cup bran or quick-cooking oatmeal to meatloaves or casseroles.
- Make muffins using oatmeal, bran, or whole wheat flour.
- Use whole cornmeal when making cornbread.

Step 2: Lower the amount of calories.

The best ways to reduce calories are to look for ways to cut down on fat and sugar. Try these tips:

- Instead of frying, try baking, broiling, grilling, or sautéing by using nonstick cooking spray or a small amount of oil.
- Use evaporated (skim or whole) milk or sour cream instead of heavy cream in sauces and soups.
- Use a purée of cooked potatoes, onion, and celery instead of cream or half-and-half as a creamy base for soups.
- Use reduced-fat cheese when possible: low-fat cottage cheese, Neufchâtel (instead of cream cheese), part-skim mozzarella, and reduced-fat sharp cheddar.
- To warm tortillas, do not fry them in oil. Instead, use a hot pan without oil, the microwave oven, or even the regular oven.
- To make flavorful refried beans, use a well-spiced sofrito instead of pork lard as a base.

- In baked goods, reduce the fat by ¼ (if a recipe calls for 1 cup of oil, use ¾ cup). You can also reduce the sugar by ¼.
- If making sweet breads, such as banana bread, zucchini bread, or pan dulce, cut the oil in half and replace with an equal amount of applesauce, mashed banana, or even canned pumpkin.
- If a recipe calls for nuts, use half the amount but toast the nuts (whole, not chopped)—this step intensifies the flavor and saves on calories.
- Replace half the eggs with egg whites, using two egg whites per egg. (If a recipe calls for two eggs, use one egg and two egg whites.)

Step 3: Cut back on high-fat meats.

- Use leaner cuts of meat: look for the words "lean," "loin," or "round" in the name.
- Use ground turkey breast in place of ground beef.
- Trim all visible fat before cooking.
- Remove the skin of poultry and put the spices directly on the meat. Only leave the skin on when grilling poultry to keep it moist.

american cancer society guidelines on nutrition and physical activity for cancer prevention

Achieve and maintain a healthy weight throughout life.
- Be as lean as possible throughout life without being underweight.
- Avoid excess weight gain at all ages. For those who are currently overweight or obese, losing even a small amount of weight has health benefits and is a good place to start.
- Engage in regular physical activity and limit consumption of high-calorie foods and beverages as key strategies for maintaining a healthy weight.

Adopt a physically active lifestyle.
- Adults should engage in at least 150 minutes of moderate intensity or 75 minutes of vigorous intensity activity each week, or an equivalent combination, preferably spread throughout the week.
- Children and adolescents should engage in at least 1 hour of moderate or vigorous intensity activity each day, with vigorous intensity activity occurring at least three days each week.
- Limit sedentary behavior such as sitting, lying down, watching television, or other forms of screen-based entertainment.
- Doing some physical activity above usual activities, no matter what one's level of activity, can have many health benefits.

Consume a healthy diet, with an emphasis on plant foods.
- Choose foods and beverages in amounts that help achieve and maintain a healthy weight.
- Limit consumption of processed meat and red meat.
- Eat at least 2½ cups of vegetables and fruits each day.
- Choose whole grains instead of refined grain products.

If you drink alcoholic beverages, limit consumption.
- Drink no more than one drink per day for women or two per day for men.

Source: Kushi, L.H., Doyle, C., McCullough, M., Rock, C.L., Demark-Wahnefried, W., Bandera, E.V., Gapstur, S., Patel, A., Andrews, K., Gansler, T., and The American Cancer Society 2010 Nutrition and Physical Activity Guidelines Advisory Committee (2012), American Cancer Society guidelines on nutrition and physical activity for cancer prevention. *CA: A Cancer Journal for Clinicians,* 62: 30-67.

index

about the authors

Maya León-Meis developed her cooking skills under her mother's guidance in her native Peru. A two-time breast cancer survivor, Maya learned firsthand the critical role of good nutrition during cancer treatment. She was inspired to produce *Maya's Secrets* after her second bout with cancer and after realizing the enormous need for health information in the Latino community. From 2006 until 2010, Maya hosted the educational television shows *Maya's Secrets* and *Los Secretos de Maya*, which allowed her to collaborate with Martín Limas-Villers and Malena Perdomo. The shows combined cooking and dance to promote good nutrition and healthy lifestyle habits. In 2011, Maya created a retooled version of *Los Secretos de Maya* to keep promoting healthy food choices. Airing on Telemundo-Denver, the show includes segments on cooking, making healthy food choices, and physical activity. The program can also be viewed at youtube.com/lossecretosdemaya11. Maya lives in Denver with her husband, Tom. They have two sons, Josh and Chris.

Malena Perdomo, MS, RD, CDE is a native of Panama. As a registered dietitian and certified diabetes educator, she is passionate about educating Latinos about the importance of good nutrition in preventing diabetes and childhood obesity. Malena's work includes counseling families and groups on lifestyle changes and disease prevention, designing nutrition education materials for Latinos, and developing video materials on nutrition and diabetes. She is an adjunct professor of nutrition at the Metropolitan State University of Denver and served as the Latino Nutrition Specialist Spokesperson for the Academy of Nutrition and Dietetics from 2005 until 2011. She was chosen by LiveWell Colorado as the *"LiveWell Colorado Nutricionista"* for her work in Spanish-language media as an educator on nutrition issues. She currently appears with Maya León-Meis on the weekly television program *Los Secretos de Maya*. Malena lives in Denver with her husband, Bill, and her two sons, Alexander and Max. To follow Malena, go to malenanutricion.com.

Martín Limas-Villers is a Mexican chef, author, and media personality. He is a graduate of the Escuela Universitaria de Hoteleria y Turismo de Sant Pol de Mar in Barcelona, where he obtained a degree in Gastronomy. Martín combines European techniques with exotic Mexican ingredients to create a unique culinary experience. After being a chef at Hotel Las Dunas, a luxury resort in coastal Spain, Martín moved to Denver to host *La Cocina de Martín*, a daily radio show that eventually became one of the most popular in the Latin communities of Denver and Phoenix. He has also appeared on television and is a regular contributor for the Denver Post. Martín splits his time between Denver and Mexico, where he recently fulfilled his dream of opening XiXim (which means "a new beginning" in the Mayan language), a restaurant with a unique and innovative take on the roots of Mexican cuisine.

Other Books Published by the American Cancer Society
Available everywhere books are sold and online at **cancer.org/bookstore**

Books for the Health Conscious
American Cancer Society's Healthy Eating Cookbook, Third Edition
Celebrate! Healthy Entertaining for Any Occasion
The Great American Eat-Right Cookbook
Kicking Butts: Quit Smoking and Take Charge of Your Health, Second Edition

Books for Children
Healthy Me: A Read-Along Coloring & Activity Book
Kids' First Cookbook: Delicious-Nutritious Treats to Make Yourself!
The Long and the Short of It: A Tale About Hair
No Thanks, but I'd Love to Dance: Choosing to Live Smoke Free

For books from the American Cancer Society about cancer and supporting people with cancer, visit **cancer.org/bookstore**.